CHRISTIAN HEROES: THEN & NOW

LOREN CUNNINGHAM

Into All the World

CHRISTIAN HEROES: THEN & NOW

LOREN CUNNINGHAM

Into All the World

JANET & GEOFF BENGE

P.O. BOX 55787   SEATTLE, WA 98155

YWAM Publishing is the publishing ministry of Youth With A Mission (YWAM), an international missionary organization of Christians from many denominations dedicated to presenting Jesus Christ to this generation. To this end, YWAM has focused its efforts in three main areas: (1) training and equipping believers for their part in fulfilling the Great Commission (Matthew 28:19), (2) personal evangelism, and (3) mercy ministry (medical and relief work).

For a free catalog of books and materials, call (425) 771-1153 or (800) 922-2143. Visit us online at www.ywampublishing.com.

Loren Cunningham: Into All the World
Copyright © 2005 by YWAM Publishing

Published by YWAM Publishing
a ministry of Youth With A Mission
P.O. Box 55787, Seattle, WA 98155

Fourth printing 2021

ISBN 978-1-57658-199-5

All rights reserved. No part of this book may be reproduced in any form without permission in writing from the publisher, except in the case of brief quotations in critical articles or reviews.

Library of Congress Cataloging-in-Publication Data
Benge, Janet, 1958–
  Loren Cunningham : into all the world / by Janet and Geoff Benge.
    p. cm. — (Christian heroes, then & now)
  Includes bibliographical references.
  ISBN 978-1-57658-199-5
  1. Cunningham, Loren. 2. Missionaries—Biography. 3. Youth With a Mission, Inc. I. Benge, Geoff, 1954– II. Title. III. Series.
  BV3705.C86B46 2003
  267'.61'092—dc21   2003008865

Every effort has been made to ensure factual accuracy. Corrections are welcome. Please understand that due to the time span and large number of people involved in the growth of Youth With A Mission, it was not possible to include all contributors or all important events in the context of this biography.

Printed in the United States of America

Christian Heroes: Then & Now

- Adoniram Judson
- Albert Schweitzer
- Amy Carmichael
- Betty Greene
- Brother Andrew
- Cameron Townsend
- Charles Mulli
- Clarence Jones
- Corrie ten Boom
- Count Zinzendorf
- C. S. Lewis
- C. T. Studd
- David Bussau
- David Livingstone
- Dietrich Bonhoeffer
- D. L. Moody
- Elisabeth Elliot
- Eric Liddell
- Florence Young
- Francis Asbury
- George Müller
- Gladys Aylward
- Helen Roseveare
- Hudson Taylor
- Ida Scudder
- Isobel Kuhn
- Jacob DeShazer
- Jim Elliot
- John Flynn
- John Newton
- John Wesley
- John Williams
- Jonathan Goforth
- Klaus-Dieter John
- Lillian Trasher
- Loren Cunningham
- Lottie Moon
- Mary Slessor
- Mildred Cable
- Nate Saint
- Norman Grubb
- Paul Brand
- Rachel Saint
- Richard Wurmbrand
- Rowland Bingham
- Samuel Zwemer
- Sundar Singh
- Wilfred Grenfell
- William Booth
- William Carey

Available in paperback, e-book, and audiobook formats. Unit study curriculum guides are available for select biographies.

www.YWAMpublishing.com

Contents

1. A Hole in the Clouds 9
2. "When God Says Go, We Go" 13
3. "You Sure Got Yourself a Preacher Here!" . 25
4. New Shoes 37
5. The Face of a Little Girl 49
6. Wave upon Wave 61
7. "You Look So Like Tom" 75
8. "You'd Be Set Up for Life" 87
9. Youth With A Mission 97
10. An Extremely Generous Offer 113
11. The First Wave 125
12. Multiplication 135
13. Hotel Golf 147
14. A Growing Mission 159
15. Only the Beginning 177
16. New Frontiers 191
17. Into All the World 207
    Bibliography 219

Chapter 1

A Hole in the Clouds

The small four-seater airplane climbed into the African sky. Twenty-five-year-old Loren Cunningham stared down at the parched land dotted with clumps of trees, excited to be on the verge of fulfilling a lifelong dream. He was on his way to the town of Kedougou, located on the Mali border. In this region, whole villages of people had never heard the gospel, and Loren hoped to preach to some of them.

Seated beside Loren, piloting the plane on the two-hour flight, was Talmadge Butler, a square-jawed, no-nonsense Texan and a veteran missionary in Africa. In the two backseats of the aircraft sat Talmadge's wife, Betty, and their young son Stevie. Talmadge was a warm, open man, and Loren had felt at ease with him from the start.

The flight went well until ominous black clouds began to appear ahead on the horizon. Whisked by the wind, the clouds soon engulfed the small aircraft. Now when Loren peered out the window, all he saw was enveloping grayness.

"Visibility's real bad," Talmadge said in his Texas drawl as he looked at his watch. "We're one hour out, and we have one hour's worth of fuel onboard. If we're going to turn around, it better be now. We can't land in this. The only safe thing is to turn back and head out of it. We can try again tomorrow."

"Whatever you say," Loren agreed. The steady beat of the rain on the fuselage was beginning to make him nervous. "I'll be glad to be out of this too."

They soon discovered that there was no way out of the storm. Although they had turned the plane around and flown for fifty minutes in the opposite direction, the storm still engulfed them, buffeting the little airplane like a cat toying with a mouse.

Loren could hear Betty praying quietly in the backseat. He turned around and saw that Stevie was wide-eyed and sitting bolt upright. Loren's heart started to race. Was this how his life was going to end—in a plane crash in Africa? He was prepared to die in the course of helping to fulfill the Great Commission, but the ministry he had been called to was just beginning. Was it going to end before it really got started?

Talmadge's voice broke into his thoughts. "Loren, this is serious. We need to pray. I can't get an accurate fix on where we are, but we have to land soon," he said.

Although Talmadge's tone was calm, Loren knew they were in trouble. They had less than ten minutes of fuel left and no way of knowing what was below them.

Loren glanced at the fuel gauge and then wished he hadn't. The needle was on empty. He bowed his head and prayed. "God, show us the way out of here. We are Your servants, and we are relying on You to guide this plane right now."

He opened his eyes, and as he looked out the window, the hairs on the back of his neck stood on end. The plane was flying right over a hole in the clouds—the first one they had encountered since being engulfed by the storm. Loren could see all the way to the ground!

"There's our opening. Keep praying. I'm taking her down," Talmadge said as he nose-dived the airplane into the gap. Loren gripped the armrests as the ground sped toward them.

"Thank you, God!" Talmadge exclaimed. "Can you believe it? That's the road leading to my runway. I think I can land her right there." With that, Talmadge pulled back on the yoke, and the plane leveled out for a landing.

The rain was still pelting down as the four passengers climbed shakily from the aircraft and ran for cover in an old hangar. Once inside, Talmadge told Loren, "That's about the closest shave I've ever had. But God sure came through, didn't He, Loren?

What are the chances of a hole appearing right there and taking us down to this exact spot?"

Loren had to agree. It was an experience he would never forget, and he had had many interesting experiences in his life so far. His mind drifted back to an experience as a four-year-old when God had saved him and his family from certain death as they served Him.

Chapter 2

"When God Says Go, We Go"

Six-year-old Phyllis Cunningham's voice belted out the words:

> Call that religion?
> No, no.
> I met a brother the other day.
> I gave him my right hand.
> As soon as my back was turned,
>   he scandalized my name.
> Call that religion?

Suddenly four-year-old Loren felt himself being jabbed in the ribs. He took a quick glance at his sister and sang out, "No, no."

A couple of families and a hobo gathered around the two young children as they sang on a hot, dusty corner of Main Street in El Centro, California, just twelve miles from the Mexican border. Tonight, May 18, 1940—a little more than a month before Loren's fifth birthday—was just like every other Saturday night Loren could remember. He and Phyllis would sing a duet, and then his mother or his father would preach to the small crowd that had gathered. Then came the best part of all. Loren's mother, Jewell Cunningham, would invite anyone who wanted to know more about the gospel to their small house on Adams Street. Waiting on the table would be the big plate of gingerbread she always made for the occasion and glasses of cold milk straight from the icebox.

Loren finished the last verse of the song without incurring another jab from Phyllis and stepped back as his father, Tom, opened his big black Bible.

Suddenly Loren's mother whispered, "Tom, we have to go right now! God's telling me we have to leave right away!"

Loren felt his mother's firm grip on his shoulder. "Come on. When God says go, we go," she said as she guided him down the street.

Loren turned to hear his father say, "That's all tonight, folks. We hope to see you at the meeting at nine o'clock tomorrow morning. You're welcome to come on over to the house right now if you want to talk some more."

With that the Cunningham family hurried along the covered sidewalk toward their car.

Although to many it may have seemed a strange way for a mother to behave, Loren did not think it odd at all. From earliest memory, both his parents had told him that God spoke to them, and when He spoke, it was their duty to obey—and fast! If Jewell Cunningham decided that God had told the family to leave, then leave they would. And leaving was not such a bad thing, Loren decided as he hurried down the busy street, because his parents always stopped for a newly invented treat on the way home—a soft-freeze chocolate ice cream.

Loren and Phyllis scrambled into their parents' brand-new black 1940 Plymouth sedan, and Tom turned the key in the ignition. The engine purred as the car pulled away from the curb.

Loren was looking idly out the window at the flagpole by the nearby gas station when suddenly the flagpole began to sway like a palm tree in a strong wind. Before he had time to think through what he had just seen, he felt a jolt.

"Oh, no. I think I've run over someone!" Tom exclaimed. The car shook again, and there was a deep rumbling sound.

"Jesus, help us, it's an earthquake!" Jewell prayed out loud.

Loren sat rooted to the spot, staring out the window. Signs hanging in store windows swung violently, and pedestrians rushed into the middle of the street. Cars came to a standstill. The rumbling grew louder. Someone screamed. Buildings shook. Loren watched as the portico covering the sidewalk where they had been singing minutes before thundered to the ground in a billow of dust. Like dominos, the buildings all along Main Street tumbled to the ground. Electrical wires snapped, sending sparks spraying into the twilight sky.

A minute later the shaking was over and the air was filled with dust, screams, and confusion.

Loren's father put the car into low gear and edged down the now rubble-strewn street. People moved slowly out of the way to let the car by. They shook their heads as they stared at what only a minute ago had been an orderly street. As Tom Cunningham drove, Loren's mother called out to people, making sure no one was hurt. The family inched their way home to Adams Street, where Tom told everyone to stay in the yard while he went inside to check out the house. Tom explained to Loren that there would be aftershocks and that everyone should stay away from buildings for several days.

Soon Loren's father emerged from the house with a large pile of quilts and pillows—and the plate of gingerbread. "No sense in letting this go to waste!" he exclaimed.

"Is the house all right?" Jewell asked.

"Far as I could tell. Nothing's broken except a few cups and plates," Tom replied.

"Thank God for watching over us," Loren's mother said. "This was a bad quake. I hope no one was hurt, but it's hard to imagine no one was, since most of Main Street is in rubble. And there's the other towns in the valley, too."

The next day Loren learned that the earthquake had been officially named the Imperial Valley

Earthquake. It had been felt as far away as Los Angeles and Arizona, and nine people had been killed in it. The dead included a woman and her daughter who had been crushed when a portico fell on them. And on the road to Holtville, the earth had opened up and swallowed a farmer, leaving behind the two mules he was leading by a rope. An entire chicken coop had disappeared into a crack that opened in the ground. Railroad tracks were bent out of shape, and bridges were damaged. One particular incident had the children in school talking about the earthquake for weeks afterward. It involved a man who had been in a hotel bathtub in El Centro when the earthquake struck. The man had been so surprised that he grabbed his hat and ran outside. It was only after he calmed down a little that he realized he was standing there naked!

Just about every building in town was damaged in some way in the earthquake, and for two weeks afterward everyone slept outside. Sleeping in his front yard made Loren start to feel like one of the hobos who lived in the park across the street. The men often came to the house begging, and Loren's mother would give them a simple task to do before feeding them a hearty meal and telling them that God loved them.

Amazingly, the Assembly of God church where Loren's father was the pastor was not damaged in the earthquake. Still, church was held outside in the parking lot the next day for fear of aftershocks. That was not the only unusual thing Loren noticed about the service that day. Many more people than normal were in attendance—people Loren had never seen in church before.

"Seems like we needed an earthquake to shake things up!" Loren's mother announced as she welcomed the newcomers. The topic of the sermon that day was on the uncertainty of life, and everyone paid close attention. When the altar call was given, many of the newcomers went forward to accept Jesus Christ and become Christians.

Eighteen months after the earthquake, another event occurred that brought home the idea of life and death, but on a much greater scale. On December 7, 1941, the Japanese bombed Pearl Harbor in Hawaii. As a result, the United States entered World War II.

Six-year-old Loren sat silently listening to President Roosevelt on the radio. "All Japanese are a threat to our society," Roosevelt said. "For their own safety and the safety of our nation, all persons of Japanese descent are to report to designated areas for transportation to internment camps."

Loren did not understand exactly what President Roosevelt was talking about, but he did understand the sad faces of the Japanese boys and girls whom he saw the following Saturday as their families held yard sales to sell off their possessions before being taken away. Loren and his mother went to one of the yard sales, and Loren watched a woman fight back tears as she sold off the family's china and furniture. His mother bought a set of pretty, aqua-colored rice bowls. For a long time afterward, whenever Loren looked at them, he thought of all the sad people who had had to leave their homes, and he wondered what had happened to them after they climbed aboard the huge covered army trucks and were carted away.

Soon after all the people of Japanese descent were taken away from El Centro, Tom Cunningham became a block warden. This meant that when the air-raid siren blew, warning of enemy aircraft, he had to patrol the block and make sure that no light was showing through the windows of houses for the enemy planes to see. It was spooky to sit in the dark listening to the buzz of an airplane overhead. Loren's mother would crawl under the bed covers with him and Phyllis and read them stories by flashlight.

Loren's father assured him that the Japanese airplanes overhead were reconnaissance planes. "They are taking photos," he said. "Those aren't planes with bombs."

Even so, it was a tense time for everyone. Loren wondered whether his dad, like many of his friends' fathers, would be called up for military service. But the government wanted pastors to stay in their churches and help the people at home get through the trials of war. So Tom Cunningham stayed put in El Centro. He hung a banner at the front of the church displaying a star for every man in the congregation who had gone off to war, reminding everyone to pray for those on the battlefield.

The trauma of war and the lingering shock of the earthquake brought many people to God during these months. Soon, in the winter of 1942, Loren was kneeling at the altar asking Jesus to come into his life too. But with such a long line of adults at the altar, no one seemed to notice him. In the end he got up and walked over to his mother. "Mama," he exclaimed, "no one's caring about me!"

Jewell embraced Loren. "Well, son, you can tell me what's on your mind."

Loren explained to her how he, too, wanted to accept Jesus into his heart, and his mother prayed with him. It was a wonderful moment in Loren's young life, and he wanted to share his newfound love for Jesus with everyone he met. Sometimes at night he lay in bed trying to figure out how to tell the whole world at once! He wished he could put big black rocks on the moon that spelled out the words, "God Is Love." But since that was not possible, he centered his efforts closer to home.

Instead of putting rocks on the moon, Loren organized a group of kindergarten and first-grade students to meet together in the Sunday-school bus parked behind the church. For days they gathered there each afternoon when school was over. One by one the children followed Loren's example and prayed for Jesus to come into their hearts and take their sins away. It seemed perfectly normal to Loren that he should give an account of the bus meetings at dinnertime, just like his parents who told about the people they had prayed with and preached to during the day.

A week after he knelt at the altar, Loren was baptized by his father. Several of the children from the school-bus meetings joined him in being baptized.

Loren's parents preached and led the growing congregation at El Centro for three more years after the earthquake. Eventually the number of people attending church each Sunday swelled to over three hundred. Much to Loren's delight, his parents had bought him a trumpet for his seventh birthday and encouraged him to join the growing church band as soon as he mastered a few notes.

Then, in the winter of 1944, Loren's parents announced to the congregation that God had called them to move to Tucson, Arizona, to strengthen a new church. Loren was nine years old by then and was not eager to leave behind his friends at school and church. He had moved several times before, but he had been too young to be greatly affected by those moves. At the time of his birth, on June 30, 1935, the family was living in Maricopa, California. Maricopa was a small town, so small that Loren was born in Taft, California, the nearest town to Maricopa with a midwife. From Maricopa his parents had moved often, pioneering several tiny churches in California, but this move would be different. This time Loren would miss riding his bike with his friends and sharing the juicy watermelons that fell off the back of the overloaded produce trucks as they lumbered through town in the summertime. It was a sober day when the family packed up their belongings and headed east for Arizona.

In the spring Loren and Phyllis started school at Flowing Wells School in Tucson, and life for the family soon settled into a new routine. Tom Cunningham preached twice on Sundays as well as on Tuesday and Thursday nights, and the children sang at street meetings. Around the same time, Loren's mother announced that she was expecting a baby, who would be born about a month before Christmas.

After only a few months in Tucson, the new church the Cunninghams were establishing had raised enough money to buy a piece of land and start constructing a church building. That is why Loren was caught off guard when the phone rang one Saturday morning, as it did ten or fifteen times every day. Everyone was seated in the living room, and as Loren's father got up to answer the phone, Loren's mother said, "Tom, if that's Pastor Elton Hill at Covina telling us he's resigning and inviting us to take his place, tell him yes!"

What a strange thing to say, Loren thought to himself as he waited for his father to pick up the phone.

Loren watched as his father put the phone to his ear and then nodded at his mother. "Hello, Elton," Tom said. "What can I do for you today?"

The conversation went on, and when it was finished, three people sat eagerly waiting to hear what had happened.

"It was just as you said," Tom began, his eyes wide. "Pastor Hill is going to resign, and he wants us to be the new pastors. I told him that if the Lord is in such a move, the church will vote for us to come without my going to 'try out' for the position."

Loren could not resist asking the next question. "Mom, how did you know that Pastor Hill would call today?"

His mother looked at him, her dark brown eyes alive with excitement. "Your daddy and I haven't seen Pastor Hill for two years, but last night as I was praying, God showed me that Covina is where we'd be going next. When the phone rang, I knew it would be him."

"What's Covina like? Is it going to be like El Centro?" Phyllis asked.

"I think it might be even better," Loren's mother beamed. "And wait until you see all the orange groves."

Loren let out a whoop. He had been in Tucson for only four months, but it had been the hottest four months of his life, and he was glad to think of going back west. And that is just what happened. A new pastor agreed to take over the little congregation and the church building program in Tucson, and the Cunningham family packed up to move once again.

As his father drove the car toward Southern California, Loren became very excited. He had been to Los Angeles several times for Christian camp meetings and rallies, but now they were going to make the area their home. Finally they crossed over the last line of hills and descended into the Azusa Valley. Orange trees laden with white blossoms lined both sides of the mile-long stretch of road from the highway to the Covina city limits. Loren drank in the scene. After spending most of his life in the desert, he was thrilled to be moving into this lush, green valley.

Soon the car pulled up at the church, and the Cunninghams peered out the vehicle's windows.

"That's our new home, right next door," Pastor Cunningham said.

Loren turned to study the wooden bungalow, which was painted white and sat on a narrow lot.

"Oh, Tom!" Jewell exclaimed, prodding her husband on the shoulder. "You joker. You told me I would hate this place, but it looks like a mansion to me!"

Me too, Loren thought. It was definitely a step up in the world from their last couple of homes.

"It's ours for as long as the Lord keeps us here," Tom said as he opened the car door. "I wonder what He has in mind for us to do here."

Chapter 3

"You Sure Got Yourself a Preacher Here!"

"John! Billy! Time for your chores," came a voice from a house down the alley.

Loren and his friends kicked the ball to each other a few more times, and then John said, "We'd better be going."

Since he had no one else to play with, Loren decided to wander home from the deserted schoolyard. His mouth began watering as he reached the top step to the house. The delightful smell of red beans, salt pork, and his mom's special corn bread filled the air. Loren headed straight for the kitchen. "How long till dinner, Mama?" he asked, suddenly aware of how hungry he was.

"About ten minutes," his mother replied as she stirred the big enamel pot on the stove, "but we're out of milk. Could you run to the widow's store and get me a couple of bottles before dinner?"

"Sure," Loren said, glad to have something to do while he waited for dinner.

Jewell Cunningham wiped her hands on her apron and went into the bedroom to get some money. "Now be real careful with this. I don't have anything smaller," she said when she came back. She handed Loren a five-dollar bill.

Loren folded the money carefully and slipped it into the front pocket of his jeans. Five dollars was a lot of money, enough for a whole week's groceries. Loren ran out the door, letting it slam behind him. His six-month-old sister Janice wailed from her crib in the bedroom.

It was a block to the widow's store, which was not really a store at all but a converted living room where a woman sold a few basic grocery items to people in the neighborhood. Loren ran up the steps and into the room, eyeing the Tootsie Rolls in the glass jar on the shelf. He took two bottles of milk from the refrigerator and carried them over to the counter.

"That's twenty cents, please," the woman behind the counter said.

Loren dug his hand into his pocket, but he did not feel the five-dollar bill. He felt in his other front pocket. Still no five-dollar bill. Then he tried his back pockets and his shirt pocket. There was no escaping it—the money was gone! It must have worked its way out of his pocket somewhere between the house and the store.

After mumbling something about losing the money, Loren left the milk on the counter, ran out the door and all the way home. His mother was feeding Janice a mashed banana when he burst into the living room. "Mama, you have to come and help me look. I lost the money. I'm sorry."

Jewell looked at Loren. "Well, son," she said, "we don't know where it is, but the Lord sure does. Let's ask Him to show us."

Right there Loren and his mother shut their eyes and prayed. When they finished, Jewell had a smile on her face. She put her hand gently on Loren's shoulder. "It's all right. God has shown me that the money is under a bush. Let's go look."

Phyllis stayed and watched Janice while Loren and his mother retraced his steps. "Jesus, You know where the money is. Please guide us to it," Jewell prayed as she walked determinedly down the alley. She stopped in front of a scrawny bush with low branches. "Let's try this one," she told Loren.

Loren dutifully stooped down. Then he spotted it. The five-dollar bill was impaled on one of the thorns on the lowest branch. "I see it!" he yelled up to his mother.

"Praise Jesus!" Jewell replied. "He never fails."

That night when Loren's father gave thanks for the food, Loren said an extra amen! He was very thankful for the food, and the milk, and the change in his mother's purse, with which she would buy the rest of the week's groceries.

Three months later Loren had another, much more serious reason to pray. This time it had to do with his father. Loren's father sometimes took short trips away from home, normally to speak at other churches or attend board meetings. This time, however, he was traveling across the country to Springfield, Missouri, to attend the national Sunday-school conference.

"Now you be good to your mother and sisters," Tom said as he ruffled Loren's hair. "You're the man of the family while I'm away."

Loren's nine-year-old chest puffed with pride. "I sure will, Dad," he said.

Three days later Loren was picking up his ball and mitt to go outside and play when the phone rang. His mother answered it, and soon Loren noticed that her voice had become uncharacteristically quiet. "I see…" he heard her say. "So the infection has set in bad and there's no point in operating? But when God is in control, nothing is hopeless. Don't you believe that, doctor?" She scribbled down a number and hung up the phone.

Turning to Loren and Phyllis, Jewell announced, "We need to pray. Your father is in serious trouble. His appendix has burst, and it's too late to operate. Peritonitis, a bad infection, has set in."

"Does that mean Dad's going to die?" Loren asked. His family hardly ever went to the doctor, so going to the hospital was a very serious matter.

"He might," Loren's mother said quietly. "The doctors can't help him, but God can. That's why we have to pray."

Loren, Phyllis, and their mother knelt on the living room floor and prayed for Tom. When they were finished, Loren crawled behind the sofa and prayed some more. He wondered what he would do if God did not save his father's life. Every week people in town received the devastating news that their father or son or husband had been killed in the war, and now his own father lay in a hospital bed fighting for his life.

The next evening one of the church members, a dour man who sold vegetables, came knocking at the Cunninghams' door. Loren watched as his mother opened it.

"I have a word for you, Sister Cunningham," the man said as he took off his hat. His voice had a mournful tone to it. "I had a dream about your husband last night; he came home in a coffin."

Loren gulped back tears.

"Thank you for coming by to tell me that, Brother," Jewell responded. "I will pray."

The vegetable man nodded.

"If God had something that important to say about my husband, He'd tell me as well as you, don't you think?"

"I guess He would," the man at the door mumbled as he put on his hat and backed down the steps.

"Come on, kids, let's pray some more," Loren's mother said as she again knelt by the sofa.

That night as Loren lay in bed, he thought about his father lying in a hospital hundreds of miles away. Was his dad dying, or was he getting better? It was a question he could not answer, but he knew one thing—when his mother asked God for things, God seemed to answer.

The next morning Loren wandered into the kitchen just as his mother was setting bowls of steaming oatmeal on the table. Phyllis was already buttering a slice of toast, and Janice was trying to worm her way out of her high chair.

As soon as Loren sat down, his mother turned to face him. He knew she had good news.

"God gave me a dream last night. In it I saw your father, and he was coming home all right—but not in a coffin. No! He was alive and wearing his pajamas on the train!"

Loren burst out laughing. What a relief! He had never seen his father wearing his pajamas outside the house.

Several days later Tom Cunningham called to say he was feeling much better and that he was on his way home by train. The family had a little party that night, with an extra helping of peach cobbler for everyone.

Two days later Loren, his mother, and his sisters were all waiting expectantly at the Pomona railroad station. A train rumbled into view and then hissed to a stop in front of them. Loren scanned the crowd. After watching several soldiers and a sailor get off, he spotted his father's burly frame.

Pastor Cunningham waved and made a beeline for his waiting family. As Tom enveloped his wife in a huge hug, Loren started to smile. His father was wearing his pajamas under his overcoat. And he was wearing his slippers, too.

Soon it was Loren's turn for a hug. How wonderful it was to feel his father's strong arms around him.

When they were finished hugging, Loren could not resist asking, "Why are you wearing your pajamas, Dad?"

Tom looked down at his clothing. "Because I was so weak the porter fixed me up with a sleeping berth on a Pullman car, and I've been sleeping for the last two days. How do I look?"

"Just the way we thought you would!" Loren laughed, recalling his mother's dream.

On September 2, 1945, the whole country celebrated. The Japanese had surrendered, and World War II was over! The Cunningham family drove to Pomona to celebrate with friends. Pastor Cunningham honked the horn all the way there, as did the other drivers on the road. Loren and Phyllis hung out the windows, waving enthusiastically at everyone.

Soldiers and sailors started to flood back into the United States. Some of them found their way to the Covina Assembly of God Church, adding to its already rapid growth. In addition to overseeing the growing congregation, Loren's father had more responsibilities within the denomination, organizing and directing other pastors and stepping in to help when churches had problems they could not solve themselves.

Life continued on for the Cunninghams in Covina until one day just after Loren's eleventh birthday when the phone rang. This time it was the Assemblies of God leader for Southern California. Superintendent Woodworth asked Loren's father to consider moving to West Los Angeles to take over a church that was in the midst of a terrible argument.

This new "opportunity" did not appeal to anyone in the family, least of all Loren. His parents promised to go and look at the church, but they came back to Covina even more convinced it was a bad situation. "We don't need to get ourselves in the middle of that mess," Loren's mother said. "And Covina is such a good place to raise children."

The next day another phone call announced that Loren's father had been unanimously elected as the new pastor of the church in West Los Angeles. This threw the Cunninghams into a quandary. They did not know what to do, but they promised to ask God about the direction they should take.

Within a week they were convinced they had an answer—not the "stay put" answer they were all hoping for but an answer that said, "Go." The family would be moving over to the much less fashionable side of the city. Once again Loren packed up his belongings, said good-bye to all his friends at school and church, and helped load up the car. For better or worse, the Cunningham family was off on a new mission.

As they drove into the area, Loren noticed that West Los Angeles was dirty and overcrowded. Since the war had ended, there was a shortage of housing, and Loren's mother had told the family that they needed to be grateful for whatever housing God provided. It was good that this idea had been firmly planted in the family's mind before they pulled up in front of Faith Tabernacle on Olympic Boulevard. The church was a large stucco building with a double-arched front door and twin towers on either side of the two-story building.

One of the church deacons met them when they pulled up and took Pastor Cunningham aside for a private conversation. When Loren's father came back, he said, "It looks like we'll be living right here, in the evangelist's quarters. Everyone grab something, and we'll head back there and take a look."

Loren helped Janice climb up the outside stairs at the back of the church. At the top was a small room with a sink, a portable gas stove, and an old sofa.

"This is the kitchen and living room," the deacon informed them. Then he pulled back a curtain. "Here is one bedroom, and there's a Sunday-school room that could do as a bedroom on the other side. Plus, if you go through that curtain there, you can get into the attic, where someone else can sleep." Then he looked very apologetic. "I am sorry to say there are no toilets up here. You'll have to use the ones in the church foyer at the back of the auditorium. And you'll have to pull that into the kitchen when you want a bath," he said, pointing to a galvanized metal tub.

Soon other church members arrived and helped the Cunninghams unload their belongings into their new upstairs home. Nobody complained about the cramped living arrangements.

"Wherever the Lord sends us, we'll be grateful!" Loren's mother said as she carried a load of bedding up the stairs.

Soon everyone was settled in. Loren had a makeshift bedroom in the attic that was curtained off from the rest of the attic. It wasn't the easiest room to get into, but it had one great feature. It was easy to get from it to the area above the main church. By crawling along beams, Loren could get all the way to the big towers at the front of the church, where he loved to sit. Through a window in the wall, he could see all the way down Olympic Boulevard. Sometimes he took his closest friends to show them his hideaway, but more often than not he kept it to himself.

While he was in his private hideaway, Loren often prayed for the opportunity to talk to people about God. Such an opportunity soon arose. Pastor Cunningham had gotten into the habit of having breakfast with Red Hamilton, the local dry cleaner who said he was not interested in Christian things. However, because Red and Pastor Cunningham had become such good friends, Red did come to church from time to time. On one occasion he even came to a special evangelistic meeting held in a large auditorium in town. At the end of the meeting, an invitation was given, asking those who wanted to become Christians to come to the front.

As Loren looked out over the congregation, he noticed Red sitting in the balcony. He made his way to the back of the auditorium and up the stairs and stood beside Red. "You have to give your heart to Jesus, Red," Loren said.

Red smiled down at Loren. "Not now, Loren. Maybe one day, but not now."

"Why not now?" Loren persisted. "What's going to be different a week from now, or a year from now? Don't you want to know peace and joy today?"

"Oh, I don't know. It's not that simple," Red replied, looking uneasy.

"What's not simple about it?" Loren asked. "You just surrender to God; He'll do the rest. Don't you want to know you are going to heaven?" Loren looked into Red's tear-filled eyes.

"Come to think of it, I guess I do," Red said quietly, tears rolling down his cheeks. "You help me, Loren."

Loren nodded and beckoned for Red to follow him. They walked down the aisle together, and then Loren prayed for Red.

Soon Pastor Cunningham came along. Red looked at him, and then at Loren. "You sure got yourself a preacher here!" he said. "I wouldn't be here except that kid wouldn't give up!"

Loren smiled. He felt proud to be described that way. His mother always said God never blessed a quitter.

Loren never quit inviting his friends to church. This was made easier because of his popularity at school. Although he was underweight for his age, Loren was agile and was soon pitching for the baseball team and playing on the football team. Loren's school, Brockton Avenue Grammar School, served a wide area of West Los Angeles, from the modest part he lived in all the way to Brentwood. Many of Loren's friends came from affluent families. Some of them were even the children of movie stars.

Loren knew that they needed to know Jesus despite their fame and affluence, and he tried to influence as many of his new school friends as possible. The following summer a plan began to unfold for Loren that affirmed his desire to share the gospel—and confirmed the words of Red Hamilton.

Chapter 4

New Shoes

"They're here!" Janice's three-year-old voice rang out from the front room. Janice had been assigned to watch for Red Hamilton's car. Red's wife and a friend of hers were going to drive Loren, his mother, and his sisters all the way to Springdale, Arkansas.

It was the summer of 1948, and thirteen-year-old Loren was about to begin an adventure he had been looking forward to for weeks. The Nicholsons, his mother's side of the family, were having a reunion. They were a lively bunch, and when they got together, they sang choruses and hymns, exchanged lots of stories, and ate homemade ice cream. Loren's mother had three sisters, Marylydia, Pebble, and Frances, and a brother named Coy. All of them except Pebble were ordained Assemblies of God pastors, and all of them were also married to preachers. Loren's grandfather, Rufus Nicholson, would also be at the reunion.

Of course, Loren did not expect this to be a family reunion like other people's family reunions. The Nicholson family reunions included a revival campaign at his Uncle Oren's church. All of the adults would take part in the preaching. His mother had been given the task of leading the youth meetings. Not only did the adults preach at church; if there were no church services being held, they would preach to each other in the house. In fact, Loren's mother told him that Grandpa Rufus had made a point of preaching to someone every single day since he was converted. Sometimes the same person got preached to over and over, but Rufus kept to his commitment.

It was a four-day trip to Springdale, and when the exhausted family finally arrived, they piled into Aunt Marylydia and Uncle Oren Paris's house. The house was located a block behind the Springdale Assembly of God church, where Oren was the pastor, ably assisted by his wife, Marylydia. The Parises had two boys, Loren's cousins Oren Jr. and Leland. Soon after the Cunninghams arrived from California, the three boys ran off to explore the local public school, which had a two-story slide down the side of the building. The slide was officially a fire escape, but it doubled as a gathering place for adventurous boys.

When the boys got back to the house, Grandpa Rufus had arrived, and later in the afternoon, Loren's Aunt Frances and Uncle Cecil Vaughan appeared on the doorstep. They lived in nearby Fayetteville, where they pastored the White Chapel Church. That night the whole family gathered on the front porch, drinking lemonade and swapping testimonies. The adults rocked gently in their rocking chairs while the children perched on the edge of the porch.

"That day you were saved, Papa. I'll tell you that's a day none of us will ever forget!" Aunt Marylydia said, sipping her lemonade.

"Tell us about it, please," Loren said.

"Well," Aunt Marylydia began, "we children were all sitting around the table one morning. Mama was fixing to put hot biscuits on our plates and pour Papa a cup of coffee. For some reason she asked him to give the blessing."

"Now that was very unusual," Loren's mom interrupted. "We'd never seen Papa pray in our whole lives. We weren't the churchy type, didn't go to Sunday school or anything like that."

"So what happened?" Oren Jr. asked.

"Instead of cursing, Papa opened his mouth to speak, but not a word came out," Aunt Marylydia said, taking up the story again. "Huge tears rolled down his cheeks, and then he started yelling, 'Glory! Hallelujah!'"

"We were so shocked we couldn't eat anything," Loren's mother interjected. "Next thing we knew Papa was running around the table hugging each of us kids. Then he saw the old hound dog at the door, and he bounded over to it and yelled, 'God bless the dog! It is Your creation!' and then he hugged it, too."

Loren looked at his grandpa, who had a big grin on his face. "Yep," Grandpa Rufus said. "I always said, if I got religion, I wanted the shoutin' kind. I guess that's what I got."

"That's what you got all right!" Loren's mother laughed. "I remember that day like it was yesterday. Soon as you calmed down enough, you set off to tell the neighbors about the love of Jesus. You were gone all day. And remember when you came home? You told Mama, 'You know, I've had a sore head from drinking too much, and I've been sore from being thrown off a horse, but in all my forty years, this is the first time I've been sore from shouting too much! My stomach's sore from laughing, too, but I thank God for the soreness.'"

Everything was silent for a moment except for the chirping of crickets, and then Loren asked, "Tell us about living in the covered wagon, Grandpa."

Loren loved to hear stories about how the family had set out in a wagon to share the gospel story with the dirt farmers in Oklahoma, Arkansas, and Texas. Along the way they had started eighteen churches. Loren's history teacher often read to the students at school about the early settlers, but when his grandfather talked about his experiences during those days, history came alive. It was hard for Loren to believe that his grandpa and aunts and uncles had actually lived before there was electricity or cars. In fact, when his mother saw a Model T for the first time, she was convinced that the radiator cap in the middle of the hood was a marker, like the sights on a gun, that the driver used to keep the car right in the middle of the road!

While modes of transport may have changed over the years, one thing the Nicholson family made plain was that the way to become a Christian never changed, and soon the whole clan was busy running the revival campaign at Uncle Oren's church. Jewell Cunningham spoke at the youth services, where she preached the same message she and her father had preached in their covered-wagon days.

At a special area-wide youth service on Monday night at Uncle Cecil's church in Fayetteville, Arkansas, Loren's mother was the guest speaker. At the end of the service, Loren knelt at the altar rail to pray. He shut his eyes. "God," he prayed, "I love you, and I am willing to go anywhere and do anything that You ask me to." Suddenly he gasped. Words had appeared in big block letters in front of him. "Go ye into all the world and preach the gospel." Loren's heart pounded as he opened his eyes and blinked several times. The words were still there in front of him!

Loren stayed kneeling at the altar for a long while, staring at the words and thinking about their meaning. He forgot about everyone around him as he promised God that he would follow the command of the words and spend his life preaching the gospel.

Finally the words faded, and Loren got up and went to find his mother. He whispered to her what had just happened, and she grinned and hugged him.

The next day Jewell left Phyllis to look after Janice while she took Loren into town.

"Where are we going?" Loren asked.

"Wait and see," his mother replied.

Soon they were standing inside a shoe store in Springdale. Mrs. Cunningham turned to the clerk and said, "This young man needs a pair of your best shoes." Then she turned to Loren and explained, "It's because of last night. The Bible says, 'How lovely on the mountains are the feet of him who brings good news.' Since you are going to spend your life bringing the Good News to others, I thought you should have a new pair of shoes to celebrate. Pick out whichever ones you like, and I'll pay for them."

Not having to consider the price tag first was something new to Loren, who soon found a pair of black-and-white wingtips he liked. His mother paid for the shoes, and she and Loren left the store.

On the way back to Uncle Oren's, Loren's mother told him about a pair of shoes she had once received. "I was about eighteen, and I was getting desperate for a new pair of shoes," she began. "In fact, my big toes had worn holes through the tops of the old shoes. But you had to make do with what you had back then, especially if you were a preacher. So I used to put the shoes on and then polish them. That way my big toes got polished black, too, and you couldn't notice the holes unless you looked carefully. But eventually the soles wore through, too, even though I packed my shoes with cardboard."

Loren tightly clasped the box containing his new shoes, glad he had never had to polish his toes. "So what happened next?" he asked.

"I started to doubt God. I heard the devil say to me, 'If God can't give you good shoes, I would just quit if I were you.' So I got down on my knees right there on the road, and I said, 'God, I won't quit! It doesn't matter if I have to go preach the gospel barefooted!' And you know what happened?"

"No, Mom," Loren replied, though he felt sure it was something out of the ordinary.

"The next day I got my answer. A friend we had met some years before sent Papa a parcel, and in it was a pair of shoes with a note that said, 'Here are a pair of shoes. They are for whichever one of your girls they will fit.' And wouldn't you know it, the only person they fit was me!"

A broad smile lit Jewell's face before she went on. "You see, Loren, if you give everything you have to God, He will make sure you have everything you need. You might have to wait a bit and resist the devil telling you it isn't going to happen, but it will come."

It was not long before Loren got the opportunity to wear his new shoes. The next day Uncle Oren took Loren aside. "I hear you're called to preach. Would you like to preach in my pulpit on Thursday night?"

Loren gulped. That was only two days away!

During the next two days, Loren spent many hours praying and thinking about what he would preach on. In the end he settled on the story in Luke chapter four. It was about the temptations of Christ in the wilderness. He prepared his sermon, and when he timed himself in his room, the sermon took about twenty minutes to deliver. But when Thursday night arrived, Loren was so nervous as he stood before the congregation that he spoke so fast he delivered the message in less than ten minutes. His mother came to his rescue, filling in the rest of the time with a few more Bible verses.

When the service was over, the twenty or so people in attendance filed past Loren and shook his hand and complimented him on his sermon. Loren had a sneaking suspicion that they were being very generous with their praise, but he did feel good inside. He had passed a milestone—his first sermon was behind him. For a brief moment he wondered about the number of sermons that might be ahead of him.

Loren stood in the warm evening air, waiting for the rest of his family. His mother came out of the church. "You did well, son," she said, ruffling his hair. "I know that wasn't easy for you, but never pass up the door of opportunity to preach. Behind every door there are two or three more opportunities, but you have to go through the first one to see the others."

When the revival campaign was over, it was time for the Cunninghams to leave Arkansas. This time they took the bus, and the journey proved just as interesting as the trip from California to Arkansas had been. Before heading west, they planned to go to Monroe, Louisiana, to meet up with Loren's father, who was preaching there. The bus route looped south through Arkansas and into Louisiana. This was the "Old South," and along the way Loren came face-to-face with segregation as he never had before. On the bus, blacks were forced to sit in the back, and they were the last ones off the bus.

When the bus pulled up to a roadside café in southern Arkansas, not only were the blacks the last ones off the bus, but also they had to go around to the back of the café to get served. There the black passengers placed their orders for food through a small window. Loren had never before seen discrimination this close up, but his mother had experienced it firsthand when, as a newlywed, she had sometimes picked cotton in the fields with black workers. Loren watched as his mother became indignant about the way the black passengers on the bus had to keep themselves separate from the white passengers.

Things came to a head when the bus driver hollered that it was time for the passengers to get back on the bus. The white passengers, who had all been served first at the café, had already finished their lunch and climbed immediately back onto the bus. But the black passengers, many of whom had had to gulp down their food because they had been served so late, straggled back to the bus.

Loren sat watching the blood vessels on the back of the driver's neck start to pulsate. When an old black man climbed back onto the bus, the driver yelled at him. "Move along, you sorry excuse for a human being. You shouldn't ought to be allowed on this bus if you can't keep to the schedule."

The old black man hung his head and shuffled along.

"I said move it, you black devil!" the driver hissed with venom.

Loren turned to see his mother stand up, take a deep breath, and step between the old man and the driver. Her voice was sharp and steady. "This man is a human being, just like you and me," she retorted, leveling her gaze at the driver. "Don't you know how much longer he had to wait to get his lunch than we did?"

Loren glanced around the bus. Most of the other passengers were pretending they did not hear the conversation, though one young man behind him was turning red. "Sit down, lady. We don't need no Yankees tellin' us how to run things down here," he finally snapped at Jewell.

"Yeah, sit down," the driver echoed, "or I'll throw you off for causing a ruckus."

Jewell did not budge an inch. "God loves him just as much as He loves you. You shouldn't be talking to him that way." She said it loud enough for everyone on the bus to get the message. Then she waited until the old man was safely seated before she sat down again.

Loren leaned over and whispered to his mother, "You could have got kicked off the bus, Mom."

"I know," she whispered back, "but some things are worth standing up for, and the dignity of every human being is one of those things."

As Loren sat watching the swamps of Arkansas and Louisiana flash past the bus window, he thought about the incident. *Mom's right,* he concluded. *Some things are worth standing up for.*

Chapter 5

The Face of a Little Girl

Back home in West Los Angeles, Loren helped his parents with an outreach to Jewish people each Saturday night in the nearby city of Santa Monica. His job was to play the trumpet, and it did not bother him one bit when his friends came down to the pier and discovered him playing gospel tunes. In fact, some of Loren's friends had become Christians as a result of Loren's sharing his faith with them and inviting them to church. One of these friends was Jimmy Abbot, a tough-talking kid who lived with his grandmother. Loren and Jimmy loved to weave their bikes down the center line of the six-lane boulevards in Los Angeles, daring the cars to make way for them. Amazingly, they were never injured on their daredevil rides.

By now the family had moved out of their cramped quarters upstairs in the church and into a spacious house on Sawtelle Boulevard. Tom and Jewell Cunningham started a Christian school, attended by 120 students, along with a children's church. Both of these ventures were new concepts to many Christians, but the Cunninghams wanted everyone, even small children, to apply God's Word to every part of their lives. Loren helped out whenever he could, though by now he had an after-school paper route to keep him busy. He was saving to buy his own car, but not just any car. He wanted a '39 Chevy, which he dreamed of painting metallic blue and lowering the suspension on. He could almost see himself behind the wheel of the car, his hair slicked back and held in place with Brylcream and his new Chippewa boots planted firmly on the accelerator.

Getting his "junior" driver's license two months before his fourteenth birthday, though, posed a problem. Because he was short for his age, Loren had to prop himself up to see over the steering wheel in the family car. This in turn meant that he had a hard time reaching the pedals. Still, he persisted until he was able to see over the steering wheel and control the pedals at the same time and thus earn his junior license. The license entitled him to drive up to the speed limit of sixty miles an hour as long as he had a licensed adult sitting beside him. Loren took every opportunity that arose to drive. One such opportunity came when the family was vacationing in the mountains. Loren's father let him drive up and down the long switchbacks as they made their way into the San Bernardino Mountains. It was an exhilarating feeling for a fourteen-year-old boy, until he noticed a black-and-white Ford in his rearview mirror. It was a police car, and its red light was flashing.

Loren eased the car to a stop on the gravel shoulder, and the police car pulled up behind him. "What did I do?" he asked his father.

"You're the driver. Get out and see what they want," was his father's reply.

Loren climbed out of the car, conscious that he barely came to the top of the door. His pants were rolled up, and he had no shoes on.

Two towering policemen stepped out of the other car. "Son, you got a driver's license?" one of them asked with raised eyebrows.

"Yes, sir, I sure do," Loren replied, reaching into his pocket and pulling out a folded permit.

The officer took it and examined it carefully. Then he handed it to the other officer. "Look at this!" he exclaimed, shaking his head. "Now I've seen everything!"

Loren climbed back into the car, proud that he was indeed old enough to drive.

Faith Tabernacle, Loren's parents' church, continued to grow and thrive, and Loren loved attending services there. In March 1950, nearly two years after the trip to Arkansas, Loren's father received some exciting news. The Assemblies of God denomination had bought an old World War II, propeller-driven airplane from the Air Force. The church christened it the *Ambassador*. The plan was to use the airplane, a Lockheed Constellation, to fly missionaries around the world. But before the plane was put to this use, the denomination decided to fly a group of American pastors around to visit the few existing Assemblies of God mission stations in Europe and the Middle East to scout out possible locations for new mission stations. The tour was scheduled to go to Rome, Greece, Egypt, Lebanon, and Jordan and finish in Israel. Israel as a country was only two years old, having been carved out of Palestine as a place for Jewish people to settle.

Loren knew that his father was eager to be a part of this mission trip and, in particular, to see Israel and walk where Jesus walked. However, the family lacked the money to send him. Then one night, two weeks before the trip was due to begin, Pastor Cunningham burst into the living room. He had tears in his eyes. "Guess what the Lord did today?" he said.

"What?" Loren asked.

"Red Hamilton heard me telling someone that I didn't think I would be going on the trip to Israel, and he told the Sunday-school class about it. They took up a special offering and raised the five hundred dollars right then and there. Can you imagine that, kids? The Lord provided five hundred dollars for me!"

"I sure can!" Loren's mother interjected with a grin. "Remember, I told you I had that dream where you were standing at the door with a suitcase in your hand. I knew the Lord would make a way for you somehow."

"I'll try to remember everything so I can tell you about it," Tom promised his family. "And I'll have the movie camera with me, so I'll be able to take lots of footage. When I get home, we'll make a show out of it. How about that, Loren?"

Loren grinned. His father always knew how to make things exciting.

The trip lasted three weeks, and Loren was at the airport to meet his father when the *Ambassador* touched down. He was eager to hear all about the adventure, and when he spotted his father's familiar suit in the crowd, he waved at him enthusiastically. After hugging his son, Tom told how the plane had taken off from Scotland on the way home but faced a stiff headwind over the Atlantic Ocean. The plane had almost run out of fuel and was forced to land at Bangor, Maine, to refuel. "I don't know if running such a huge plane as that is something the Assemblies of God should be involved in," he concluded. "The whole planeload of us were praying like we'd never prayed before when the pilot told us the fuel was running low!"

"Well, you made it," Loren replied, "and I can't wait to see the movies you shot."

During the next few days Loren watched the movies as his father wrote a narration to go along with the footage.

As it turned out, though, the event that impacted Pastor Cunningham the most was not recorded on film. Instead, Loren learned about it in church as his father spoke about the trip. He was sitting two rows from the front of the auditorium and only half listening when his father began describing the event. Suddenly Loren realized that the church had grown unusually quiet. It was then that he noticed his father's voice was cracking with emotion.

"One afternoon," Pastor Cunningham began, "while we were in Jerusalem, a pastor friend and I decided we would head for Bethany to find the tomb where tradition says Lazarus was laid. We easily found it and the Arab man in charge of it. While he was fumbling with the padlock on the gate, a little Arab girl, maybe eight years old, came up to us. I guess she was from the Palestinian refugee camp we had passed. She was holding a sleeping baby with her left arm. She stuck out her right hand and said, 'Baksheesh.'

"We had been in Israel long enough to know that she was begging for money, and we had been warned to discourage begging by ignoring such pleas. But I couldn't do it. You would have needed a heart of stone to ignore the look of desperation in the little girl's eyes. There were traces, too, of the eye disease that eventually blinds many poor Middle Eastern children.

"By now the gate was open, and the guide and the other pastor were climbing down the stone steps into Lazarus's tomb. The guide became impatient, but I stayed by the gate long enough to drop a small coin into the girl's hand. It was probably worth about seven American cents, but the little girl's face lit up like our children's faces do at Christmas, and she thanked me and hurried away."

Loren looked around at the familiar faces of the congregation. Everyone was still paying rapt attention to his father as he continued, tears now rolling down his cheeks.

"I climbed down into the tomb, and then we paid the guide and made our way back to our hotel room. I didn't think much more about the little girl. I'd seen hundreds of children begging from tourists along the route of my journey. However, later that night, as I knelt beside my bed and prayed, the memory of her came back to me. I thought of her look of expectation that I could do something for her. I wanted to tell her that I had only a few cents to offer her and that what she really needed was Jesus, the Bread of Life. As I thought about the hopelessness of her life without Christ, I started to weep. I couldn't get her face out of my mind.

"Later that night I made a vow that when I came home, I would challenge all of you in this church, and every church I preach in, to take the gospel to every place and every people on earth. *World missions* used to be just a couple of words, but not anymore. From now on world missions has a face, and it's the face of that little girl."

Loren wiped a tear from his eye and looked around to see many other members of the congregation doing the same thing. It was obvious that somehow this little girl had deeply affected his father.

Over the next year, Loren accompanied his father many times as he showed the movie of his trip and spoke the commentary that went along with it. At the time, a movie that showed Europe and Palestine after the war was still a novel experience, and Tom was invited to show his movie not only in churches for miles around but also to Lions and Rotary clubs.

It was not long before Loren knew by heart every scene in the movie and the narration that went with it. And just as his father had vowed in the hotel room in Jerusalem, wherever he went, he told the story of the little Arab girl and the need to saturate the world with the gospel message. Loren heard the story scores of times, and it never failed to impact him, until one day he, too, wanted to be a part of taking the gospel to the ends of the earth. It was as if the verse he had seen before him while kneeling at the altar in his uncle's church in Springdale was coming alive to him. Go into *all* the world!

Under Pastor Cunningham's leadership, Faith Tabernacle turned over more and more money for use in furthering overseas evangelism. Week after week Loren's father told him what an amazing thing was happening. Despite all they were giving to missions, nothing else in the church budget was suffering. In fact, the overall giving in the church went up by 30 percent, and all the bills were easily taken care of.

Loren was not surprised, then, when his father challenged the church to give even more. For weeks

The Face of a Little Girl 57

after his father's return from Europe, Loren heard him speak of a missionary in Africa named Paul Bruton. After hearing about Paul so much, Loren felt like he could almost feel the dust that swirled around the missionary's home and taste the manioc root he ate for dinner. Then, unexpectedly, Loren, along with the rest of the church, was given an opportunity to see the Jeep the missionary was going to drive—if the church paid for it, that is!

On the particular Sunday morning, the congregation arrived for the morning service to find the church doors locked. Inside Pastor Cunningham was keeping the doors closed until the last moment. Finally he unlocked them, and the surprised congregation filed in. An even bigger surprise awaited them inside. Loren, who was the first one through the door, gasped when he saw it. Somehow his father had managed to maneuver a brand-new red Jeep through some double doors and right inside the church. The vehicle was now parked in front of the first row of seats!

Tom Cunningham was always coming up with something new, such as a covered-wagon ride to bring children to Sunday school or a Texas barbecue and roundup to attract the neighbors. But a Jeep inside the church? Loren felt his father had outdone himself this time.

When the surprised congregation was seated, Pastor Cunningham stood and explained what the Jeep was doing at the front of the church. "Paul Bruton needs a new Jeep, so I borrowed this one from the local dealership for you to see for yourselves what it looks like. If we dig deep enough and ask the Lord for creative ways to make money, I am confident that we could send this Jeep." He turned around and patted it on the hood. "Yes, we could send this Jeep all the way to Natatingu, West Africa! What do you say?"

The congregation erupted into applause. When the noise died down, Pastor Cunningham added, "And while we are sending it off, we might as well fill it with food and supplies for Paul and the other missionaries, don't you think?"

Another round of applause erupted from the congregation. Then Loren heard his father say, "Let's all stop right now and ask God how He wants us to be involved in this project."

Loren bowed his head. He looked down at his expensive Chippewa boots, the ones he planned to impress the girls with when he drove his '39 Chevy down the street, and a question popped into his head. *How can I spend my earnings on a car for myself when there is a Jeep right in front of me that a missionary in Africa needs to reach people with the gospel?*

Loren knew the answer. In God's economy the Chevy was a luxury, the Jeep a necessity. Right then and there he decided to give the next two months' income from his paper route, which totaled forty dollars, to the Jeep fund. Many others in the church made similar sacrifices, and in two months the Jeep was paid for, filled with supplies, and on a ship bound for West Africa.

Loren did not regret giving his wages to help make sending the Jeep possible, but once it was purchased, he asked his father if he could take on two extra summer jobs so that he could save up for the Chevy. Soon he was working at a local restaurant washing dishes and at the "Chicken Call In" as a delivery boy. All the extra effort paid off, and by the end of summer, Loren had his dream car. It was not in the best shape: the rear doors were held in place by wire, and the eleven-year-old body had rust spots. But Loren and his friends attacked the vehicle with vigor. In no time they had it sanded down and painted the shade of blue Loren had had in mind for so long.

As this restoration work was taking place, Loren was looking forward to driving the car around but not quite as much as he had thought he would. The story of the little Arab girl his father told was fixed firmly in his mind. Loren knew that one day, soon perhaps, he would go out into the world and preach the gospel himself.

Chapter 6

Wave upon Wave

Loren's first opportunity to share the gospel message outside the United States came two years later, in his last year of high school. It was Easter vacation, April 1952. A businessman had offered his two vans for an evangelistic trip, and there were spaces for twelve young men to travel in the vans across the border into Mexico. It was an unusual idea, just the sort of thing that appealed to Loren, who was very excited when he was asked to join the group. All of the other team members were a year or two older, college students, but Loren felt confident that he would fit right in. He had filled out and grown tall in the years since starting high school. He had learned some Spanish in school and had taken part in street meetings since before he could remember.

The plan was for all of the young men to take turns at street preaching, even though their Spanish was not perfect. Much to Loren's surprise, it did not seem to matter. Even when preaching in their high-school Spanish, they would attract a crowd, and when they gave the invitation to accept Christ, men and women would kneel right in front of them in the dirt and pray.

To save money, the young men slept in sleeping bags out in the desert. Loren tried not to think of the snakes and spiders that might inhabit the area, but he never imagined that the real danger would come from bullets! On the second morning in the desert, the young men woke up to the sound of gunshots. Thankfully, they all stayed lying down as they tried to figure out what to do next. All sorts of explanations raced through Loren's head. Was this like the persecution he had read about in the New Testament? Or was some man angry that his wife or daughter had become a Christian after listening to the Americans? Loren did not know the answer, but he did know it was time to crawl to the vans and climb in without being shot.

Once all twelve of them were in the vans, they took off at a high speed. Loren looked out the window and noticed two Mexican men with rifles cocked. The men were target practicing! Soon the entire vanload of young men was laughing. It was not persecution after all, just two men who did not know the Americans were there, shooting at cans.

Over that Easter break about twenty Mexican people asked to accept Christ into their lives. Loren talked and prayed with many of them and marveled at how God could use someone from another culture to reach into a person's life and touch that person with the gospel.

During the trip Loren and two of the other young men came down with dysentery and ended up spending a few hours in a hospital on the border. But this did not dampen Loren's enthusiasm for cross-cultural evangelism.

As they drove back across the border, Loren began to wonder whether at some time in the future he might enroll in Bible college and join his father as a pastor. For now, though, he had more immediate plans. Loren had worked hard in high school and earned enough credits to graduate in December 1952, six months ahead of his class. Having graduated from high school early, he was eager to get a job and make some money to pay for college, since his parents could not afford to pay for it themselves. And if he had any money left over after paying for college, Loren had dreams of trying his hand at investing. He took a full-time job at Ralph's, where he soon worked his way up from packing groceries to working in the produce department, trimming and stacking fruit and vegetables.

That summer Loren took two courses at Santa Monica City College, and then in the fall he enrolled at the nearby University of California at Los Angeles (UCLA). He lived at home to save money and kept up his job at the grocery store. He also traded in his '39 Chevy for a more reliable '48 Dodge. By midway through his first year at college,

Loren had saved enough money for the down payment on a four-bedroom house! The house, located in Anaheim, cost $9,995, and Loren's mother cosigned the mortgage. Loren rented out his new purchase. At eighteen years of age, he had become a landlord. Loren liked investing in land, and he soon found another bargain, a lot near a resort lake that he also purchased.

After his first year at college, Loren decided that he was ready to leave home and that now might be a good time to go to Bible college. He settled on attending Central Bible Institute, the Assemblies of God Bible college in Springfield, Missouri. Since it would cost more to attend there than to live at home and go to UCLA, to make up the difference, Loren sold his house and lot, along with a second car he had purchased, making enough profit to pay his tuition and his room and board. His sister Phyllis, who was a year ahead of him, decided to transfer to the Bible college as well, and soon the two of them were planning the fifteen-hundred-mile trip east.

Everyone, including nine-year-old Janice, helped load up the green '48 Dodge. When it came time for the two to head out, Pastor Cunningham gathered his family together and prayed for Loren and Phyllis. It would be the longest the family had ever been separated, and by the end of the prayer, tears were streaming down everyone's cheeks.

The Dodge held up well during the trip to Missouri, and Loren felt at home from the moment he arrived in Springfield. He had listened to his grandfather tell many stories of pioneering Assemblies of God churches. Now he recognized some of the students' names. These young adults were the children and grandchildren of some of the early converts his grandfather had led to the Lord.

Loren found it easy to comply with the rules of the college. There were rules against card playing, dancing, gambling, and drinking alcohol—the same standards his mother had insisted on in their home. He did not waste a single minute being homesick. Now that he was in Bible college, Loren intended to make the most of it. He joined the college choir and made many friends. He and Phyllis often went on double dates.

Loren found a small rural community called Green Hill that had an old, abandoned church. He and a classmate decided to take turns preaching in the church and see if they could bring it back to life. After a few weeks Loren's classmate left, but Loren rounded up other young people to help him. One served as the youth pastor and another the Sunday-school superintendent, while Phyllis was the music director. Soon Loren was preaching each Sunday to a thriving congregation of about fifty people.

As Christmas rolled around, Loren and Phyllis wanted to go home for the holiday, but neither of them had any spare cash for a bus or train ticket. Loren prayed hard and looked for a solution to their problem. It came in the form of the Carpenter Bus Manufacturing Company in Mitchell, Indiana.

The company was situated 350 miles northeast of the Bible college. Loren had heard that the company sometimes needed drivers to ferry new school buses out to California. He came up with an idea. If he drove one of their buses to California, he could drop off a number of his friends along the way and earn himself and Phyllis a free trip home and $150 for their return trip.

Loren contacted the company and arranged to drive one of its buses west. All went well on the trip, and he and Phyllis enjoyed a wonderful Christmas at home in California with their parents.

Upon Loren's return to Central Bible Institute, a senior student named Art Gast invited him to become part of a vocal quartet. The group needed a tenor, and Art had noticed that Loren had a strong and versatile voice. Loren readily accepted the invitation and began practicing with the group. The young men sang in local churches and planned to travel that summer from coast to coast, singing and evangelizing. This meant that Loren needed to hand over the leadership of the Green Hill Church to a married couple and students who were staying in Missouri for the summer.

Loren had a wonderful summer traveling around, singing, preaching, and seeing the sights. At the end of the tour, he took the time to visit his folks and then headed back to Missouri for his junior year in college.

All went well during this year except for the trip home for Christmas. Once again a bus needed to be delivered to Los Angeles, and Loren was happy to drive it there. He collected the bus in a blizzard, only to find the vehicle's vent was stuck open. Loren and his companions nearly froze on their way west. But by the time Christmas Day rolled around, Loren was laughing with his family about the experience in the comparative warmth of Southern California.

Not long after Loren returned to college, his mother sent him a *Herald Express* newspaper article. Loren's heart sank as soon as he saw it. There was a photo of a man being carried away in a stretcher and the headlines "Drug Dealer Shot by Police." The man in the photo was his old biking buddy, Jimmy Abbot. Loren knew that Jimmy had drifted away from the church and gotten involved in smoking, drinking, and then finally selling drugs, but it saddened him to read how he continued to mess up his life. On the eve of his wedding, Jimmy had done a drug run and been caught. Instead of stopping, he had run from the police, and an officer had shot him in the back. Now, the article said, if Jimmy lived at all, it would be as a paraplegic. As hard as it was to admit, Jimmy had made his choice and wasted his life.

Loren could not help but think of another friend of his and Jimmy's, Donny Bennett. It seemed like just yesterday when they had been at high school together and Loren had sat in his Chevy for three hours urging Donny to accept Christ as his savior. Donny told Loren that he thought it was a good idea to become a Christian one day when he was older, but it was not something that he needed to do right now. The following week Donny had been murdered near the railroad tracks. The case was never solved, but it had left Loren with a sense of how short life was and how everyone makes his or her own decision about God.

Loren folded the newspaper article and tucked it into his bedside drawer. He knew he would continue to pray for Jimmy, and he hoped he would get to preach to thousands of other Jimmys before they ended up in the same terrible situation.

Phyllis graduated that spring and returned home to Los Angeles to attend the University of Southern California. Loren did not go home for the summer. Instead the King's Magnifiers, as the quartet called themselves, planned an extensive tour that would take them all the way to the Bahamas and then up the east coast of the United States and on to Montreal, Canada. Their first stop, in the Bahamas, would be twenty-year-old Loren's first trip "overseas."

As he sat in the twenty-five-seater airplane, listening to the drone of the engines, Loren looked down at the aqua blue ocean. Scattered below were small, irregular-shaped islands, some of them no bigger than a football field, others stretching for several miles. All of them were fringed with impossibly white beaches. But it was not the beaches Loren and the other members of the quartet had come to see. It was the thousands of Bahamian people who lived on these scattered islands.

The group stayed at the home of an American missionary in Nassau and took trips to the other islands to sing and preach. Apart from the fact that they were on an archipelago and the weather was a sticky ninety-five degrees, to Loren there was little difference between this trip and the many other trips the quartet had taken during the college year. That is, until a Wednesday afternoon about five days into the trip as he was preparing to preach to about two hundred youth. Loren closed the door of the guestroom he was staying in and knelt beside the bed to read his Bible. As he flipped through its pages, he asked God to speak to his mind, a practice his mother had taught him as a small boy. What happened next was anything but normal.

Without warning, a huge map of the world appeared in his mind's eye. Loren blinked, but the map was still there. Not only that, it now started to move. Large waves began rolling onto the continents of the world. They splashed onto the shores of Central and South America and then rolled on over the continent to Australia and then to Asia and Europe. As soon as one wave got under way, another one started behind it. Soon the entire map was covered with ocean waves beating on every shore. Then suddenly the waves turned into the faces of young people flowing to every corner of the world and across every nation.

As quickly and as unexpectedly as it had appeared, the picture left. But Loren stayed on his knees, contemplating the amazing event that had just taken place. And as he thought, one question played in his mind: *What was that about?* Loren began to wonder whether somehow he had been given a glimpse of the future. Perhaps God intended for waves of young people, with all of their zeal and enthusiasm, to be sent out to every continent and every country until they covered the whole world. It was a big thought to take in at once, and if it was true, it led Loren to another, even more bizarre thought. Why would God have given *him* the picture? If it was true, what part was *he* going to play in sending waves of young people out around the world?

Although the quartet still had five more days in the Bahamas, Loren found it hard to think about anything but the moving picture he had seen in the guestroom. Ever since his father's experience with the little girl begging by the tomb in Israel, the Cunningham family had been heavily involved in mission projects. Many missionaries had stayed in their home, preaching on Sunday and leading outreaches into the community. These missionaries had come from many places around the world, but they all had two things in common: they were all older, and they all had professional qualifications. Loren knew how strange it would sound to people if he told them that he thought God intended to send hundreds, thousands, and then millions of young people out around the world to preach the gospel. He decided not to tell anyone what he had seen until he himself understood how it would be possible.

A week later, as the quartet traveled to Miami to continue their tour up the East Coast, Loren was still thinking about his experience. The group checked into an inexpensive hotel, and they were about to go out to dinner when Loren remembered something. The last time he had heard about his Aunt Arnette she was living in Miami. *Perhaps she's only a few miles away from me,* Loren thought as he looked out the motel window. *What would she say if I tracked her down?*

Loren knew that most aunts would be glad to see one of their nephews, but his father's family had split nearly thirty years before. His father sometimes spoke of the split with a crack in his voice. Loren's Grandfather Cunningham had been converted later in life, just as Grandpa Nicholson had, and had become a preacher. When Loren's father was five years old, his mother had died of smallpox. It was a traumatic event for the entire family, not only because their mother died but also because the local health department came to the Cunningham house and insisted that all of their personal belongings be burned to stop the spread of the infectious disease. In a single day the Cunningham children lost their mother and all their material possessions. Heartbroken but undeterred from his preaching, Loren's grandfather had sworn he would continue with his itinerant ministry. One by one the five children were placed in various foster homes around Texas, where they worked for their keep. Loren's father lived in seven different foster homes, some of them better than others.

The children were no longer together, and two of the three girls, Sandra and Arnette, grew bitter toward their father's religion. They wanted nothing to do with a God who they thought took first their mother and then their father away from them. They stayed close to Tom Cunningham, though, until he announced that he, too, was going to become a preacher. The older girls told their nineteen-year-old brother that if he pursued such a foolish course, they would never speak to him again. Loren's father began preaching, and Sandra and Arnette kept to their word.

This had all happened twenty-nine years before, and it was why Loren was not sure where his aunts lived or what they did. He had heard that Aunt Arnette was a rich businesswoman who had remained single and that Aunt Sandra was married. Three years earlier, when Grandpa Cunningham died, Loren's father managed to track down Arnette, but she had mocked his efforts and announced that she would not even cross the street to attend her father's funeral.

Now, as Loren sat alone in the motel room, he opened the drawer and took out the local phone book. He scanned down the "Cu" column until he came to Cunningham. Cunningham, Arnette. There it was, staring at him in black and white, the address and phone number of an aunt he had never met. Loren became aware of his pounding heart and sweaty hands. What should he do? Was there any point in calling his aunt and being insulted as his father had been? Or might his aunt be the tiniest bit curious to meet a nephew she had never seen? Loren did not know, but he was sure of one thing—if he did not call, he would always wonder what might have happened. He picked up the phone and with trembling fingers dialed Arnette Cunningham's number. He heard the phone ring and waited for someone to answer.

Chapter 7

"You Look So Like Tom"

"Hello." It was a refined woman's voice, not one Loren had ever heard before but still vaguely familiar.

Loren took a deep breath. "Hello, I'm Loren Cunningham. My father is Thomas Cecil Cunningham. I think I am your nephew, and I am wondering if I could meet you."

Loren stopped talking and waited for a reply. The other end of the line was silent. Finally Aunt Arnette replied, "No, you can't. I'm too busy!" And with a click she hung up the phone.

Loren sat for a long time and stared at the pattern on the bedspread. At least he knew the answer to one of his questions. It was definitely his aunt, even if she had not wanted to talk to him. By the following day Loren had to admit just how frustrated he was by the short phone conversation. He decided to try to talk to his aunt again. This time he planned out what he wanted to say.

Once again Aunt Arnette answered the phone, and Loren launched in. "Hello, this is your nephew Loren again. I don't want to be a bother to you, but I'll be leaving Miami tomorrow and I was wondering if I could see you for a few minutes."

This time Aunt Arnette seemed ready for him. Her clipped voice said, "I'm sorry, but my employees are throwing a birthday party for me this afternoon. I don't have time to see you."

Loren was not surprised when she hung up on him again. In fact, he was a little encouraged. She had said two whole sentences to him this time. And now he had a little more information. Today was her birthday. Loren set out down the street in search of a gift store. He bought a pretty linen and lace handkerchief and a birthday card. He planned to try to deliver them to his aunt the following day on his way out of town.

The next morning the quartet loaded up their station wagon and prepared to leave Miami. Before they headed north, Loren asked if he could stop at a phone booth on Biscayne Boulevard. There he dialed Aunt Arnette's number one last time.

"Hello, it's Loren again," he said when she picked up the phone. "We are headed out of town, and I have a birthday gift I wanted to drop off for you. I have only a few minutes. I won't come in. I just want to meet you."

He could hear a deep sigh at the other end. "Well, I suppose if you must," his aunt replied.

Ten minutes later Loren found himself parked outside an impressive house in one of Miami's better neighborhoods. He got out of the car, and as he walked up the path, a woman came out to meet him. Loren soon found himself looking into a pair of gray-blue eyes that were remarkably like his father's.

While he was studying his Aunt Arnette, she was evidently studying him. "You look so like Tom when he was your age," she said, and Loren thought he could detect a little wistfulness in her voice. "The same smile, same big frame. You are a little taller though, aren't you?"

Loren nodded as he studied this immaculately dressed woman with the diamond rings and manicured nails.

Loren stood at the front door and explained that what he had said on the phone was true: he had only a few minutes, since the others were waiting for him in the station wagon.

Suddenly Aunt Arnette said, "You have another aunt. Compared to her, I am a pauper. I just talked to her on the phone, and she said she would like to see you. How far north are you traveling?"

"All the way to Montreal," Loren replied.

Aunt Arnette was silent for a moment. "Well," she said cautiously, "if you are interested in meeting your Aunt Sandra and your Uncle George, she has a summer home in upstate New York. She should be there this time of year. Do you have an itinerary?"

Loren reached into his jacket pocket and pulled out a sheet of paper and the birthday card and gift. "Happy birthday," he said with a smile. "And here's a list of the places we'll be staying. I'm sorry, but I really have to go now."

Loren and Arnette shook hands, and Loren walked back to the station wagon alone.

Five days later Aunt Arnette tracked Loren down to tell him that Aunt Sandra was sending her limousine to pick him up at the church he was visiting in Montreal and drive him to her summer home on Lake Placid.

Loren recalled Aunt Arnette's words, "Compared to your Aunt Sandra, I am a pauper." Once the limousine arrived, he understood exactly what she had meant.

Years before, Aunt Sandra had married George Meehan, a business tycoon who made his money from textile mills in the Northeast and then turned to investing to further enlarge his fortune. Loren's first impression of Aunt Sandra was that she reminded him a lot of his sister Phyllis. They had the same gray eyes and lilting laugh. Aunt Sandra seemed more at ease with Loren than Aunt Arnette had been, perhaps, he thought, because she'd had longer to adjust to the idea that he was coming to visit.

The summer house Aunt Sandra lived in on Lake Placid was beyond anything Loren had ever dreamed of. As his aunt showed him around, Loren lost count of the number of bedrooms and bathrooms in the place. Aunt Sandra explained to him that *Better Homes and Gardens* magazine had been out to take photographs and write an article—not on the mansion itself but on their boathouse!

It seemed that Aunt Sandra and Uncle George had just about everything they could want. Loren did not like to ask, but he gathered they would have dearly loved to have had children of their own.

The visit went well, although Loren was a little worried that he might break something or use the wrong fork at dinner. Everything was so formal, so rich, and he could not help but think of the contrast this was to his aunt's impoverished upbringing. It was hard to imagine that when she was a teenager, this dignified and sophisticated woman had had to earn her keep by hard physical labor. Loren was very impressed with the way things had turned out for her.

When the visit was over, Aunt Sandra invited Loren to return anytime he wanted. "There's obviously plenty of room in the house for one more!" she laughed. Loren had to agree.

The rest of the singing tour of the East Coast went by fast, and Loren soon found himself back at college for his senior year. However, Loren had been so busy singing and preaching all summer that he had been unable to work and save money to pay for his last year of tuition. Since he knew that his parents did not have any money to spare, he asked God to somehow provide the money he needed.

Three days before the fees were due, Loren was praying down by a creek behind the college. His prayer was that God would provide his financial needs. When he had finished, Loren walked past the administration building. "Loren, Loren," he heard someone yell. He turned around to see the secretary with her head poked out the window. "You have a phone call," the secretary said, once she had his attention.

Loren bounded around to the front of the building and picked up the phone.

"Hello, Loren dear, it's your Aunt Sandra."

Loren was very surprised. "Hello," he replied. "How are you?"

"I'm just fine," she said. "I tracked down this number because I wanted to tell you something. I have decided to pay for your last year of tuition at college. I am sure you need some kind of help, don't you?"

"Well, yes, my fees are due in three days, and I don't have them yet."

"Just as I suspected!" she laughed. "Well, consider them paid. Give me a mailing address and tell me how much they are, and I'll get a check off to you today. In fact, Uncle George and I have decided to set up a trust for you so you can have all the education you need."

"Thank you," was all Loren could think of to say. This woman who had only been a name to him and who had no time for religion was going to pay his way to finish Bible college!

Loren gave his aunt the address and the amount of his fees and hung up the phone. By now the shock had worn off, and he let out a whoop of joy. He felt joy not only because his fees were paid but also because his aunt's heart was softening toward her long-rejected family.

The school year of 1956–1957 flew by for Loren, who was selected as president of the student body. Being president involved many meetings and social events. On top of this, Loren took more than his share of courses, so that by the end of his senior year he had graduated with two degrees, one in Christian education and the other in theology. In addition, he continued to travel with the quartet, and by the end of the year, they had visited all forty-eight states in the Union. Loren did not like to remain idle!

As valedictorian Loren had the honor of giving a speech at his graduation ceremony. His parents and twelve-year-old sister Janice came to Missouri for the occasion.

Loren chose 2 Timothy 1:5–6 as the text for his speech. "When I call to remembrance the unfeigned faith that is in thee, which dwelt first in thy grandmother Lois, and thy mother Eunice; and I am persuaded that in thee also. Wherefore I put thee in remembrance that thou stir up the gift of God, which is in thee by the putting on of my hands."

When Loren had finished reading the verses, he looked around at the crowd in the auditorium. He spotted his parents smiling from the front row, and he noticed several other people he knew dotted throughout the audience. Then he launched into his speech. He talked about how his Grandmother Nicholson had embraced the gospel and how she and her husband, as well as his Grandfather Cunningham, were among the Assemblies of God's pioneer workers. Then Loren talked of the untiring faith and good works of his mother and father and how he hoped that the legacy would continue on to his generation.

By now Loren's father was pastor of the First Assembly of God at Long Beach, California. He had been called there to help heal relationships after a nasty church split. In 1957 the church was back on its feet and looking for an associate pastor. The church asked Loren if he would consider the job, working under his father as the assistant coordinator of the education, youth, and music departments. Since Loren could not think of anything that he would like more than working with his father, he gladly accepted the position. He used the education fund Aunt Sandra and Uncle George had set up for him to enroll at the University of Southern California to get another bachelor's degree and a master's degree in education.

At the church Loren was in charge of the choirs that Janice and Phyllis sang with. It was a wonderful situation. Loren also moved back in with his parents. His mother's corn bread never tasted so good.

Loren had been at the church only six months when he noticed one Sunday morning that his father seemed shaken during the sermon. It was not until after lunch, when the family was finally alone together, that Loren got to talk to his father about it. "Is everything all right, Dad?" he asked.

His father shook his head. "I've been in ministry for twenty-six years, and I don't question the Lord, but I sure would like to know what's going to happen," he replied.

"Spit it out, Tom. What did the Lord tell you?" Loren's mother asked in her usual direct manner.

"Well," Tom began in a choked-up voice, "I was just enjoying the choir and getting ready to speak when a still, small voice whispered to my heart, 'Two weeks from today you will be reading your resignation from that pulpit.'"

Loren sat quietly. Although he believed every word his father said, it was hard to think that his father would be resigning from the church they had all come to love, and in just two weeks!

Sure enough, a week later, in early March, the Southern California District Council of the Assemblies of God convened in Los Angeles. On the third day Tom Cunningham came home amazed. He had been elected Assistant Superintendent of the Assemblies of God of Southern California. He explained to Loren that his new position involved promoting world missions, the thing that had become closest to his heart.

The following Sunday Loren listened as his father read his resignation from the pulpit. Pastor Cunningham also announced that he would be leaving the Long Beach church and moving closer to the Southern California Assemblies of God headquarters. Loren knew that his father had made this decision for more than personal convenience. Tom Cunningham believed that when a pastor was through somewhere, he should move on and give the congregation the opportunity to relate to the new pastor. When the new pastor did arrive, he asked Loren to stay on. But Loren, too, felt it was time to let the church adjust to life without the Cunninghams.

Loren, Janice, and their parents found a hillside home on West 61st Street to move into. To have a little more independence, Loren claimed the room above the garage as his bedroom at the new residence.

In the summer of 1958, Loren accepted an assistant pastoral position at the Inglewood Calvary Assembly as the musical director, youth director, and Christian education director. It was a daunting task, as Inglewood had one of the best musical reputations in the country and Loren felt the burden of maintaining such a high standard. Still he loved his work at the Inglewood Calvary Assembly, and soon he had several choirs taking turns singing on Sunday mornings.

A happy family event took place that August. Loren's sister Phyllis married Len Griswold, a navy jet pilot stationed in San Diego. The two of them seemed made for each other.

After the wedding Loren began to wonder when he might be getting married. It did not seem like it would be anytime soon. At Bible college he'd had lots of dates, but no one seemed quite right—not that he was sure what "quite right" was! He did know that any young woman he brought home would have to have a sense of humor to accept his mother's well-meaning but sometimes blunt words. She would have to have something else, too—flexibility. Although Loren was happy being an assistant pastor, he had the nagging feeling that God was about to take his life and turn it upside down. If that were the case, he would need a wife who could handle a lot of changes.

The more Loren thought about his future, the more convinced he was that it had something to do with the waves of young people he had seen moving across the world in prayer in the guestroom in the Bahamas. Of course he had no idea how it would all begin to work itself out.

Chapter 8

"You'd Be Set Up for Life"

That same fall Loren signed up for a philosophy of religion course at USC. The course included lively discussions, and it did not take long for Loren to realize that he was the only Christian in the class. How different the atmosphere was from Bible college! Yet Loren felt confident that his faith could stand up to whatever the course had to offer.

A few weeks into the course, the professor abruptly stopped lecturing one day, pointed at Loren, and asked, "You are a Christian. Do you believe in miracles?"

"Absolutely I do," Loren replied.

"Why?" the professor questioned.

Loren thought for a moment. He sensed that the entire class was listening intently. "Let me tell you a story. I was twelve; my father was a pastor, and we had an evangelist come and preach in our church. I was sitting in the front row when a woman on a stretcher was brought in. I had seen a few dead people in open caskets during funerals at the church, and I could see that this woman was close to death. Her skin was gray. I could see the outline of her bones through her dress, and she was hardly moving. I watched her shallow breathing, thinking that I might actually see the moment of death.

"The visiting preacher and my father came up to her and laid their hands on her forehead and prayed, asking Jesus to heal her. The next thing, I saw her bolt upright, jump off the stretcher, and run around the church like she was on some kind of autopilot. Then she came back to the front and started jumping up and down with joy and energy that couldn't be explained.

"That week my dad got a letter from her doctor, who said that the woman had been riddled with cancer and had only hours to live. Now the doctor had run every test on the woman, and she was completely cancer-free. So when you ask me, 'Do you believe in miracles?' I have to answer, 'How can I not believe in them?'"

"You have a point," the professor said abruptly, and then went on with his lecture.

After class was over, the professor came up to Loren and invited him to dinner. He explained that his wife was very interested in miracles and that she would love to hear more of Loren's stories.

"You'd Be Set Up for Life"

The dinner went well, and after that the professor invited Loren to come to his office to talk some more. This time several members of the senior staff of the philosophy department, including a professor who had recently transferred to USC from Duke University, joined them. They all spent the afternoon discussing miracles. When the meeting was over, the professor asked Loren to stay for a few minutes after the others had left. Loren did not have a clue what he might want to talk about next.

"You know," the professor began, "we don't get many Christians through this program, and we certainly don't get many who are as articulate and sure of their beliefs as you are. I have a proposition for you. If you stay on here for your Ph.D., I can offer you an associate professorship, and once you're finished, I'll make you a fully tenured professor of philosophy."

Loren was speechless.

The professor went on. "It's a great position, the starting salary is generous, seventeen thousand dollars a year, and there's a raise every year. You'd be set up for life."

"Thank you, sir," Loren stammered, amazed at the confidence the professor had placed in him, "but I can't accept your offer. God has given me a call to work with youth and missions, and nothing is more important to me than that."

As Loren drove home that evening, he thought about the astonishing offer. The words "You'd be set up for life" echoed in his mind. He would be set up for life, that was for sure, but was it the life God was leading him to? No, he concluded. God had a plan for his life, and it included young people and missions. He just wished he had a bit more information than that to go on.

The more he thought about it, the more convinced Loren became that God wanted him to expose young people to overseas missions. One night several weeks later, Loren stood up at a youth meeting that included young people from many different denominations and said, "I have an announcement to make. We have been doing a lot of fun activities as church youth groups, but I think we should also be thinking about doing something constructive to help others." Loren looked around to make sure everyone was paying attention. "I am thinking of taking a group of you on an overseas trip, not to see the sights but to be evangelists."

A gasp went up from the hundreds of young people who had gathered in the auditorium.

Loren was excited. "We are considering Mexico. If you think you might be interested in a trip like this, for evangelism and not tourism, raise your hand."

A sea of hands waved in the air.

"Okay," Loren continued. "You start praying about it and talking with your parents and pastors. If you want more information, leave your name and address on the table at the back of the auditorium."

When Loren checked, over two hundred names were on the list. Now that he knew that many young people were interested in a mission trip, Loren began to explore their options. His first idea was to charter a ship to go down the coast of Mexico and maybe even to South America. However, the more he worked with his travel agent, the more complicated the whole scheme became.

Finally the travel agent said to Loren, "You know, Pastor Cunningham, it would be much simpler to hire a plane and take a hundred kids to Hawaii. It's foreign enough, and since it just got statehood, you won't have to worry about passports or visas."

"You have a point there," Loren replied. "I'll pray about it."

The more Loren prayed about the idea, the more he felt that that was what God wanted him to do. The youth group liked the idea too. Some in the congregation, however, questioned what a group of young people could do in a missionary setting. After all, they didn't have any Bible-college training or practical skills to offer. However, Loren's father helped calm their fears. He was widely known as "Mr. Missions" by now, and he was willing to stand with Loren and see what impact young people could have in a cross-cultural situation.

Other people were concerned about the workload that Loren was putting on himself. Loren was in charge of so many ministries at church as well as working on his master's degree. When people asked him, "Aren't you worried that you are going to wear yourself out and have a breakdown, with all the things you are doing?" Loren always gave the same answer: "No. I want to see how far I can stretch myself."

During spring break 1960, Loren and 105 young people climbed aboard a DC6 prop airplane to make the thirteen-hour flight from Los Angeles to Hawaii. They were met at Honolulu Airport by a local youth group and whisked off to lead a church service. They had practiced dramas and songs before they left California, and as they flew from island to island, many young Hawaiians responded to their enthusiastic presentations.

Loren was concerned about some in the group, though. It was to be expected, he supposed, that a few of them would see the trip as an opportunity to scout out new dates or get a suntan on the palm-fringed beaches. So Loren decided that the next time he led a trip like this, he would be clearer about the purpose of the trip and the fact that an outreach was not the place to just hang out. It was a mission, one that used young people as the missionaries!

All in all, Loren was pleased with the way the trip went. The young people from California had made many friends among their Christian counterparts in the Hawaiian Islands, and he was sure that they would continue to breathe new life into their youth groups when they got home. As he sat on the airplane returning to California, Loren thought about the young men and women who had blossomed as a result of the challenging situations they had all been through. What they needed, he concluded, were more ways to stretch themselves, to test their limits and their faith. And Loren was determined to blaze a trail for them.

In July 1960 Loren sold his car, left his position at Inglewood Calvary Assembly, found the cheapest round-the-world airfare he could buy, and set off. His plan was to scout out missionary opportunities for youth. His first stop was Hawaii, where he had been only weeks before with the youth group. From there he took a flight out across the western Pacific Ocean. After a brief refueling stop on Wake Island, the plane landed in Tokyo, Japan, where Loren preached in a Bible college and a few churches before continuing on to Hong Kong.

The highlight of his stay in Hong Kong was the opportunity to climb a hill in the New Territories and look out into China. There was no way that he could travel into that country. Communist China did not issue visas to Americans. However, it was a thrill for Loren to be able to stand and pray for this country that was shrouded in so much mystery.

From Hong Kong Loren took a Pan Am flight to Saigon, Vietnam. The flight was one that Loren knew he would never forget. Although no one in the United States talked about it much, the Pan Am crew was well aware that a guerilla war had broken out in the region. When Loren noticed that the plane was staying very high instead of descending steadily for landing, the steward told him that they were trying to avoid ground-to-air fire! Eventually the pilot managed to bring the plane down for a safe landing, and a relieved Loren disembarked the aircraft.

Everywhere he went in Vietnam, Loren took notes on the needs of the people and any effective Christian work he saw being done. After three days he flew on to Thailand and Cambodia and then on to India.

In Delhi Loren looked up a missionary couple his father knew. The couple had a grown son named Ken, who had been born and raised in India. Loren was impressed with the way Ken spoke the language and knew the local customs. On Loren's second night there, Ken took Loren for a walk. They looped around behind a bazaar area and into a large, open field where several fires smoldered. A sickly smell hung in the air, and many people milled around.

"Do you know where we are?" Ken asked.

"No," Loren admitted.

"This is a burning ground. Come over this way."

Loren followed Ken as he skillfully made his way through the throng. Soon they were standing near a huge pile of sticks. It was dark by now, but a man illuminated the scene when he touched a torch to the pile. The flames licked high into the air, and Loren saw the silhouette of a teenager's body on the top of the pile.

"Let's stay back here and watch," Ken said as he pulled on Loren's shirtsleeve. They took a few steps backward.

"They are talking about the boy," Ken said, his ear turned toward the crowd gathered around the fire. "Apparently he was killed in a knife fight this morning."

Loren stood in the shadows and watched the flames engulf the young body while a priest circled the fire and chanted prayers. Wailing filled the air.

When he got back to his room, Loren could not get the picture of the funeral pyre out of his mind. He guessed that in his life he had probably been to a dozen funerals, but they were the funerals of church members. Even the most tragic of these services had some element of hope to them. But he had just heard the wailing of a family without hope for their child. He wished he could stay right there in India and get to work, but something called him on.

Loren's next stop was Pakistan, then Egypt, Lebanon, and Jordan, and then the Holy Land, where he toured Israel. Even though Loren had never been there before, he felt as though he could have given a tour himself. He had sat through his father's movie so many times, he knew exactly where he was at all times. Loren was particularly impressed with Galilee, which, after the noise and hubbub of Jerusalem, was so peaceful.

After walking in the steps of Jesus, Loren continued westward to Turkey, Greece, and southern Europe, where he visited many churches in which his father had contacts. Everywhere he went, he was confronted with needs. If the world were to be reached with the gospel, he concluded, it would take all Christian churches working together.

Finally, after traveling through Europe by train on a Eurorail pass, going into communist Berlin,

Scandinavia, and Great Britain, Loren decided it was time to return to the United States. His heart was bursting with all of the needs he had observed. He had to find a way to meet at least some of them. Loren still did not quite know how he was going to go about doing this, and he certainly had no idea that his passion to help others would set him on a roller coaster ride like nothing he had ever experienced before.

Chapter 9

Youth With A Mission

Loren allowed himself only a few days' rest before setting out again. This time he was off to speak to youth groups and churches throughout California to tell people about the needs and opportunities he had seen on his trip around the world. Everywhere he went, Loren was struck by the number of bright, enthusiastic young people who were fired up by his message but who could see no way to actually get to or stay on the mission field. The frustration Loren felt over this seemed to culminate one evening at Stan's Restaurant in Bakersfield, California.

Following a meeting at a Bakersfield church, two young men, Dallas Moore and Larry Hendricks, had taken Loren to the restaurant for a sandwich. They made small talk for a while, most of it centered on Dallas's pride and joy—a 1956 two-toned aqua-and-white Chevy Bel Air, which Dallas kept in mint condition. Loren recalled a time when he could talk endlessly about the plans for his own cars, but now the sights and smells of the world encroached on those dreams. He found himself wanting to impart to these two twenty-year-olds sipping milkshakes beside him the need that existed for people to go and share the gospel.

"You know," Loren began, "before I left on my trip, I knew about most of the things I was going to see. I had helped my father with a movie commentary on Israel, and many missionaries had stayed in our home and described the way they lived. But actually looking into the glazed-over eyes of a begging child with a bloated belly, or standing in the shadows watching as a sixteen-year-old boy's body was burned and listening to his mother's wailing cry...well that's so different from hearing about such things from a comfortable, padded pew in California."

Loren watched the faces of Dallas and Larry. *Yes,* he thought, *they are with me.* He continued, "The really great thing is that there's so much we can do to make a difference out there!"

Dallas took a gulp of his milkshake and looked into Loren's eyes. "I see what you mean," he said. "I don't doubt that there are a lot of needs out there, but they're for people who've been trained as nurses and doctors and Bible college graduates, and stuff like that." He looked over at Larry. "The two of us operate heavy equipment like backhoes and bulldozers. I can't imagine us on the mission field." Then he smiled.

"I guess you have a point there," Loren replied. "But I wouldn't give up so soon. I'm sure there must be a place you are needed."

Over the next several weeks Loren thought a lot about his conversation with Larry and Dallas. Something about it bothered him, though he could not put his finger on what it was. That is, until a month later, as he was driving down Pacific Coast Highway with two of his friends from Inglewood Calvary Assembly. Their names were Bob and Lorraine Theetge, and although they were around forty, they shared Loren's youthful outlook on life.

As Loren sat in the backseat of the car, he thought about the thousands of young people he had talked to since arriving back from overseas. So many of them were eager to do something for the Lord on the mission field. Loren had even received a few letters from some of the people he had talked to who had signed up for Bible college as a first step in the process.

A first step, Loren thought. *That's the problem.* Bible college was the first of many steps it took before people could go. But how many obstacles would they encounter along the way? Some of them would get married at Bible college and settle down; others would not be able to raise the level of support they would need to go overseas or would be rejected by their mission boards. But what else could they do?

Loren looked out at the waves of the Pacific Ocean crashing just a few feet from the car. Suddenly, without warning, the "problem" of all those fired-up young people merged with the vision of the waves he had seen in the guestroom in the Bahamas, and Loren understood the connection. His mind began to spin.

"Bob, Lorraine, listen to this!" he said. "What if we started an organization to help young Christians, not from just one denomination but all young people who love the Lord, to get out onto the mission field? We could recruit them right out of high school, before they go on to college, send them overseas somewhere where they could do something meaningful for a month or a year, and then challenge them to find a way to go back for full-time service."

"It sounds interesting," Lorraine said. "How do you think this would be financed?"

Loren's mind continued to swirl with ideas. So many things he had thought about for years were coming into a single, laserlike focus. "We would show them how to sacrifice, trust God, and raise their own support. That way there'd be no limit on how many could go! What do you think, Bob?"

Bob glanced back at Loren from behind the steering wheel of the car and said, "Let's do it!"

The words reverberated inside Loren's head. *"Let's do it!"* It wasn't "You do it" or "Great idea; someday someone will do it," but "Let's do it." Loren now had a clear direction and two other people to partner with. The possibilities whizzed through his head. "First we'll need something to mail out to all the youth pastors whose churches I've visited since I got back."

Loren, Bob, and Lorraine went straight to work transforming Loren's bedroom into an office. To make room for a desk, Bob gave Loren a brown leather sofa bed that replaced Loren's regular bed. Another friend gave him a desk and an ancient typewriter. Then they set up a mimeograph machine that Loren had unearthed in a back room at church.

A month or so earlier Loren had been featured on a local Christian TV series called *Men with a Mission*. Now, as he thought about what to name this new endeavor, that name came back to him. Loren wondered whether Youth With A Mission would be a good name for the group. The more he thought about it, the more he liked it. It was simple and direct, and it said it all: they were youth, and they had a mission. Loren asked both the Theetges and his parents what they thought, and they all agreed it would make a fine name. There was just one problem: it was a bit cumbersome to say. The name was soon informally shortened to YWAM (pronounced *why-wham*).

In his denomination, Loren had twenty-five presbyters over him, and they gave him their unanimous backing as he set up the new interdenominational mission. Lorraine typed a letter to pastors, telling them that Loren was setting up a way to funnel young people out onto the mission field and asking them for a list of young people from their churches who might be interested in learning more about the opportunities ahead. Of course Loren was not yet sure what all of these opportunities were, though he had noted that the Far East Broadcasting stations in Hong Kong, Tokyo, and Manila were looking for able young workers, and he thought that might be a good place to start.

Soon 180 mimeographed sheets of paper bearing the seeds of an idea were in the mail. Loren, Bob, and Lorraine sat back and waited for a response.

Within days Loren heard of a missionary in Liberia who was trying to get a road built through the jungle to a leper colony. Immediately the conversation with Larry and Dallas in Bakersfield popped into his mind. Here was a job that needed skilled bulldozer operators!

Loren got on the phone and tracked down Dallas right away. The conversation went well, up until the point where Dallas asked who was going to pay for his ticket and living expenses. Loren explained that he and Larry would need to raise the money themselves, either from their own savings or through asking their church and other Christian friends to support what they were doing. At that stage all of the enthusiasm drained out of the conversation, and Dallas told Loren that he would get back to him in a few days.

They were anxious days for Loren, who was concerned that he might be asking too much of Dallas. But then Loren consoled himself. This was not some harebrained scheme he had thought up.

It was something that God had been showing him over the past four years. One way or another, it had to work. Besides, Loren was not asking anyone to do anything different from what he was doing. His only income was made from the occasional speaking engagement and the money a few family members and friends gave each month. Lorraine was doing the office work for free.

Finally Dallas called back. He explained that he had discussed the idea with his parents and his pastor, and they were right behind it. He also said that he had talked to Larry, who was eager to go as well. Loren let out a sigh of relief.

"But what about the money?" he asked.

"That's taken care of, Loren," Dallas replied. "I'm going to sell my Chevy."

"Praise God" was about all Loren could think of to say. He knew how much the aqua-and-white car meant to Dallas.

The ball was rolling. Other young people were writing and calling to ask if they also could be sent somewhere, and Loren began to wonder whether there were other opportunities in Africa. Since everything in the office was running smoothly, he decided to go and see for himself.

As Loren settled in for the transatlantic flight, he thought about how different this trip was from the previous one. Then he had been searching for a way to get people to the mission field. Now YWAM was a real mission with two missionaries preparing for service. The whole plan was beginning to unfold like a map. While Larry and Dallas, two American Christians, were in the final stages of preparing to go off and help Liberian lepers, Loren could see past this to a time when Christians from *all* nations would be recruited and sent to people from *all* other nations. *From all nations to all nations,* he thought. *That has a good ring to it.*

When Loren had the chance to speak to a group of young Ibo people in Nigeria, he explained his vision of youth going out to preach the gospel and challenged the people to take up the call. As soon as the meeting was over, a Western missionary at the gathering rushed up to Loren. "You can't go around saying that!" he said indignantly.

"Saying what?" Loren asked.

"You know, telling the Nigerians that they should be missionaries," the missionary retorted. *"We* are the missionaries, and *they* are the natives."

Loren smiled and shook his head. "As far as I can tell, their Bible says the same thing as ours does," he said as firmly and as politely as he could. "And that Bible tells us to go into all the world and preach the gospel to all people."

The Western missionary did not say much about it after that, and Loren continued to challenge the Christians to whom he spoke to take the gospel to those who had not heard it. He called his message *Taking the Gospel from Every Nation to Every Nation,* and he preached it to Christians everywhere he went.

Loren's next plane trip was in a four-seater aircraft. A veteran missionary from Texas, Talmadge

Butler, was to fly Loren to Kedougou, two hours away on the Mali border. Talmadge's wife, Betty, and their young son Stevie were accompanying them on the trip. Everything started out fine until Loren spotted ominous black clouds in the distance. Soon a brisk wind was buffeting the plane.

As the clouds engulfed the airplane, Talmadge had a hard time seeing where he was going. Finally, after they had been flying for an hour, he decided they should turn around and head back where they had come from. They had set out with only two hours' fuel on board the plane, and now they had just enough to make it back to the airfield they had left from.

Talmadge turned the plane, and they headed back. Another fifty minutes went by, and they were still engulfed by the storm.

Loren could hear Betty praying quietly in the backseat. He turned around and saw that Stevie was wide-eyed. Loren's heart started to race. They were in serious trouble. They had to land within the next ten minutes or risk running out of fuel and crashing, but they were still socked in by clouds and could not see the ground to find a place to land. Although Talmadge seemed calm, Loren could tell he was worried, too. By now the fuel gauge showed empty.

Finally Loren prayed. "God, show us the way out of here. We are Your servants, and we are relying on You to guide this plane right now."

When he looked out the windshield, he could scarcely believe it—they were flying right over a hole in the clouds, the first one they had encountered since being engulfed by the storm. Loren could see all the way to the ground, where there was a narrow dirt road. Talmadge nose-dived the airplane into the gap in the clouds as Loren gripped the armrests. The ground came speeding toward them.

"I think I can land her right there," Talmadge said as he pulled back on the yoke and leveled the plane for a landing.

The wheels of the small craft thumped onto the narrow road as everyone aboard let out a sigh of relief.

"Thank you, God!" Talmadge exclaimed. "Can you believe it, Loren? This is the road leading to my runway. We're home, and we're safe!"

"Yes, thank You, Lord," Loren agreed as Talmadge guided the plane down the road, onto the grass runway, and into a weather-beaten WWII hangar, out of the raging storm. Talmadge stopped the engine, and the four of them climbed out of the aircraft. As the four of them huddled in this shelter that had room for little more than one small plane, Talmadge told Loren that it was one of the closest shaves he'd ever had. But God had helped them through the emergency to safety.

Loren agreed. It was an experience he would never forget. Nor would he forget it three days later when, after finally making it safely to Kedougou, he preached there. Talmadge had arranged for a Muslim man to translate Loren's street preaching into the local tribal language. The first night Loren preached, the Muslim translator became convinced that Loren was speaking the truth and asked to become a Christian.

The following day Loren's host offered to take him to a remote village called Bantiko. As far as the missionary could tell, the villagers there never had visitors and had never heard the gospel. Loren became very excited when he heard this. He was finally going to preach to people who had absolutely no knowledge of Jesus or the Bible. He wondered how they would receive him. What would he say to them? And was there something he and the people of Bantiko had in common that he could use to help open the villagers' hearts to the gospel?

Four men set out for Bantiko: the missionary, Loren, a translator, and a local boy whose job it was to stand on the hood of the jeep and guide the driver through the tall jungle grass. As they bumped along, Loren felt like he was on an adventure straight out of one of the missionary adventure books he had read as a boy.

When they had been traveling for a while, they came to a river and stopped beside it. The group would cross the river on foot, wading waist deep. Loren spied a man on the other side of the river, darting among the trees. Soon the man disappeared into the jungle.

"He'll be off to warn the chief that we are in the area," the missionary said. "Let's hope they are in a mood to welcome us."

Soon they walked into a clearing. "This is Bantiko," the missionary announced.

Loren looked around. He saw a dignified man with white hair and a white beard standing in the middle of the clearing ahead. The man carried a walking stick woven from horsehair and had a stern expression on his face. The missionary walked over and greeted him with a traditional African handshake, which entailed grabbing thumbs and clicking fingers. Loren followed his example, and the chief relaxed.

"I have come a great distance to give you a wonderful message," Loren said. Then he waited while the translator translated his words for the man.

"Really?" the chief asked. "What kind of message?"

"A message your whole village needs to hear," Loren replied.

The chief thought for a moment, and then he summoned another man and gave him some instructions.

"I have called everyone in from the fields," he said.

Loren smiled. For some reason he noticed a nearby rock with a brown stain on it. "What is that for?" he asked, pointing at the rock.

"It is where we sacrifice chickens," the chief replied. "It keeps the evil spirits away."

"Oh," Loren replied, thinking about how he could use that information in his talk.

Half an hour later a group of people from the village were sitting cross-legged in the clearing. Loren started by pointing at the sun and saying, "I want to tell you about the God who made the sun, and the moon, and the earth." The young man interpreted, and the chief nodded in approval. Loren went on. "This God has sent me to you to give you a great message. I see that you understand that blood must be shed as a sacrifice, but I ask you this: how can the blood of a chicken pay for human sins?"

Loren could hear a hum of voices as the villagers tried to answer the question. When the hum died down, Loren told the people how God had sent Jesus to die on the cross as a sacrifice for their sins. Smiles of relief spread over some faces, and some of the people applauded as Loren continued with his message. When it was over, Loren asked who wanted to accept Jesus. The chief and about half of the villagers present nodded and then prayed with Loren.

Back across the river, as the Jeep wound its way through the jungle grass, Loren sat in awe of what had just happened. It seemed incredible to him to think that he, a young American man, had just introduced Christ to a group of Africans who had never before heard the gospel. The missionary was also astounded and promised to go back and help the villagers start a church.

Next Loren made his way to Liberia to the leper colony where Larry and Dallas were due to arrive in a few weeks. Then it was on to Ghana and Togo. From there Loren was scheduled to take a train to Sokode, Dahomey, where his next missionary host lived. However, when he stepped off the plane in

Togo, he could hardly see straight. The runway came in and out of focus as Loren collected his bag. By the time he reached the airport fence, Loren knew he was very sick. He had to lie down before he passed out.

Loren spotted a one-story hotel and willed himself to walk to it. The manager gave him a key, and Loren stumbled into the hotel room. The room had nothing in it but a bed, but that was all Loren needed. He dropped his suitcase, kicked off his sandals, and flopped onto the bed. The room spun around in front of him, and then everything went black.

When Loren regained consciousness, he wasn't sure how much time had passed—perhaps a couple of days. He awoke shivering with cold, even though he could see the sun shining through the window. He knew he must have malaria. He was incredibly thirsty, and he forced himself to get up and stagger out into the public area of the hotel in search of something to drink.

After a few hours and some bland food, Loren felt well enough to continue his journey, this time by train to Sokode. His host in Sokode asked him if he would like to go to the village of Natatingu. Loren could not quite think of where, but he knew he had heard that name before. When he reached the mission house, he remembered. Standing outside the house was an old red Jeep, but not just any red Jeep. It was the same red Jeep that Loren had helped purchase ten years before, when he donated the money he had been saving to buy his own first car.

Tears welled in Loren's eyes as he walked over to the vehicle and inspected it. He could picture the Jeep parked at the front of the church as if it were yesterday, with his father standing beside it asking the congregation to sacrifice their earnings to send it to the mission field. The vehicle was shiny and new then. Now it was scratched and dented but still serviceable. Loren asked the missionary if he would take a photo of him beside the Jeep to send home to his parents. He smiled as he thought of the thrill it would give them to see their son, a real missionary, standing beside the mission Jeep.

Loren's next stop was Umaiaha, Nigeria, where they needed a substitute teacher for a local Bible college. Loren volunteered to fill in as teacher for the term. He enjoyed getting to know the African students, and as he had done before, he challenged them to take the gospel into all the world. Two of the young men took up the call and made plans to move to Sierra Leone when they graduated. That fact alone made the entire term worthwhile for Loren.

In October, just as Loren was getting ready to leave Nigeria, he received a letter from his father describing Larry and Dallas's send-off at Los Angeles International Airport. *Yes,* Loren thought, *Youth With A Mission now has two official missionaries in the field.* It wasn't yet waves of young people, but the first trickle had started. Loren's father also wrote that four other YWAMers were preparing to join the Far East Broadcasting Company (FEBC) in Hong Kong, Tokyo, and the Philippines.

Soon afterward another letter arrived. The envelope and matching paper had a curly embossed *M* in the left corner. *Just Aunt Sandra's style,* Loren thought as he tore open the envelope. The letter from his aunt asked Loren to visit her and Uncle George on his way back from his trip. She said they had something important to discuss with him.

Loren was glad for the invitation. Relationships within the Cunningham family had improved greatly since he had contacted his two aunts. In fact, only months before, Aunt Sandra and Aunt Arnette had enjoyed a wonderful reunion with their siblings. It was the first time Tom Cunningham had seen his two sisters in twenty-nine years, and they all promised to stay in contact.

After living on two dollars a day for the past several months, Loren looked forward to some of his aunt's hospitality. He knew her chef would cook him anything he asked for, and a king-size bed awaited him. As he sat aboard the TWA flight winging its way to New York, Loren relaxed and imagined the luxury that lay ahead. He had no idea that his aunt was about to propose an idea that would test his determination to reach the world.

Chapter 10

An Extremely Generous Offer

Loren sat propped up in the luxurious bed, a breakfast tray on his lap, the morning newspaper in his hands. He put the paper down and took a sip of orange juice and a bite of bacon. This certainly was the life! For a brief moment he wondered how different things might have been if his father and Aunt Sandra had not parted ways all those years ago. Would he have spent his school vacations in this mansion—or maybe out on their luxury yacht sailing the Caribbean? Would Aunt Sandra have driven out to visit them in her Cadillac? Loren smiled at the contrast. How funny that would have been—a Cadillac parked outside their two-room attic home above the church in West Los Angeles. Loren could not imagine Aunt Sandra climbing those stairs and down again to wind her way around to the front of the church to use the public bathroom. As it was, the entire church building could easily fit inside the Meehan mansion.

A dog yapped outside the bedroom door, bringing Loren back to the present. He finished his breakfast, skimmed the front-page and international news, and then got up. He knew his aunt wanted to talk to him around ten o'clock.

It was just past that hour when Loren walked down the marble staircase, through the French doors, and out onto the terrace, where he knew his aunt would be waiting. He took a deep breath when he saw her. For some reason he felt strangely nervous this morning.

Aunt Sandra turned and kissed Loren on the cheek. "Did you sleep well?" she asked.

"Fine, thank you," Loren replied as they walked over to the wrought-iron garden furniture. Aunt Sandra sat down and beckoned Loren to follow. Her butler Hawkins appeared with a tray bearing serving items and a steaming pot of tea.

After Hawkins had poured the tea and retreated from the terrace, Aunt Sandra cleared her throat. "Loren, dear," she said, "Uncle George had to go off to work early, but I know I speak for both of us. We were...well, let's get to the point... We were wondering if you would consider coming to work with Uncle George. You could learn how things are done in the business."

Loren took a deep breath. So that was what Aunt Sandra wanted. What an offer. Aunt Sandra had never had children, and Loren knew that implicit in the offer was the idea that one day he would inherit a fortune. He rubbed his hand across his chin. What could he say? It was a generous—an extremely generous—offer. *If* he took it, he could move right into the mansion, drive around in the Cadillac, and one day become a multimillionaire! But it was a big *if*. To accept the job, Loren would have to turn away from his dream of sending young people out around the world. Larry and Dallas would be the first and the last Youth With A Mission missionaries to go out.

As he looked into the hopeful gray eyes of his aunt, Loren struggled for the right words to tell her that God had called him to do something different, and he had to follow His will. Loren was painfully aware that his aunt and his father had had a similar discussion thirty years before, when Sandra and Arnette had offered to help him with his schooling. When his father refused their offer, telling them that he had been called to preach, it had led to nearly three decades of pain and separation. How would his aunt take it this time? As rejection? Would she respond with scorn and sarcasm? Loren did not know, but he did know that he had to find the right words to turn her down gently.

"Let's go for a walk down by the shore," Loren finally said, hoping this diversion would give him enough time to come up with the right words. They strolled down toward the water's edge, and Loren began to speak. "It isn't that I'm not extremely grateful for your offer, Aunt Sandra," he said.

Her eyes locked on his. "But you are saying no?" she retorted.

"I can't do it," Loren continued, reaching out to touch her hand. He tried to explain about his time in Africa and Youth With A Mission and how he hoped one day to be sending young people all over the world.

Aunt Sandra listened silently, and when he was finished, she said, almost pleading, "Loren. Couldn't you work in the United States? That way maybe you could work with the business and do your missionary work, too. There are lots of people right here who need help, you know."

"I know, Aunt Sandra," Loren replied. "And I am very sorry, but I just can't stay. God has given me a vision for the world, and I can't confine it to just one place, no matter how much I'd like things to work out."

After a long silence, Loren's stomach turned as he waited for his aunt's response. Finally she spoke in a low, clear voice. "You know, Loren, our family has been torn apart too much." She smiled bravely. "Let's make sure that doesn't happen again. Good luck with your new work. Let me explain it to your Uncle George. I don't think he'll understand, but I'll do my best."

"Thank you," Loren replied. "I don't ever want us to be torn apart again either, and I truly appreciate your offer. It's something I will never forget."

Aunt Sandra squeezed Loren's hand. "You are so much like your father." Her voice broke as she spoke, and Loren knew that she meant it as a compliment.

Later that day Loren flew back to Los Angeles. He was very relieved that Aunt Sandra wanted to keep the family together no matter what. It had certainly made things less awkward when he left her.

Once he arrived home, he had a lot to do. Four YWAMers, two young men and two young women, were in the final stages of preparing to go and work with FEBC in Hong Kong, Tokyo, and the Philippines. Loren helped them raise support by speaking in their churches, and soon they, too, were on their way.

By now a woman named Mrs. Overton had joined Lorraine in the office. Although she was quite elderly, she had the energy of a young person—along with excellent office skills. Mrs. Overton recruited a dozen other senior citizens who helped with office duties and prayed regularly for YWAM. Soon Loren and Lorraine did not know how they had managed without her.

Loren continued to speak in churches and at youth rallies around California. The year flew by, and soon Larry and Dallas were back from their year's commitment in Liberia. Things had gone well for them. In addition to building the road to the leper colony, they had helped establish two churches across the river in Ivory Coast. As Loren listened to their stories and watched the glow in their eyes, he realized that their work in Africa had done as much for their faith as it had for those in Liberia they had been working among. Loren longed to get more young people out onto the mission field so that they, too, could experience the faith-building excitement of sharing the gospel and helping others.

The work of Youth With A Mission continued at a fast pace, though Loren found he still had time to daydream. And for some reason he could not quite explain, his daydreams turned more and more toward a young woman he had met while preaching at a church in the San Francisco Bay Area. He did not know why he couldn't get Darlene Scratch out of his thoughts. Darlene was the only child of Pastor Ed and Enid Scratch, and she had not been very friendly when she accompanied her parents to lunch with Loren after church one Sunday.

Although Darlene had the most vivid blue eyes and honey-blonde hair, the day she met Loren she had been dressed in one of the least flattering dresses he had ever seen. She had asked a couple of questions during the meal, but she had had little to say afterward as her father drove them all back to the now empty church parking lot.

Loren did not know what to make of it when Darlene walked toward her car. It was a black '39 Ford hotrod with a lowered front end! It seemed so out of character with the quiet girl he'd just had lunch with.

As Darlene got into her car, she gave Loren a mischievous smile, and he realized there might be more to Darlene Scratch than she had let him see so far.

Loren decided he wanted to see this young woman again. When Loren learned that Darlene was going to be in Los Angeles visiting her cousin, he called and asked her to go out with him while she was in the area. She accepted, and Loren drove to the airport to meet her. This time Darlene had upgraded her outfit to a pretty lemon-colored suit, and she was much more interesting, though still a little reserved. Somehow Loren sensed that this was not the real Darlene, either, and so the second time they went out together, Loren decided to get to the bottom of things. After a nice dinner together, he drove Darlene to a spot overlooking the city and parked the car. He looked over at her and said, "I know we don't know each other that well, but is there something you need to tell me?"

Darlene's piercing blue eyes met his. "I like you, Loren. You are a really good friend."

"You are about to say 'but,'" Loren interrupted.

"Yes," Darlene agreed. "There was someone in my life..." She looked out the window at the city below them and kept talking. Loren listened attentively as she explained that she had wanted to be a missionary from the time she was nine years old. It was then that she had seen a vision of herself surrounded by Asian children. She had gone to nursing college to prepare for overseas work, but then a young man had shown up and swept her off her feet. He was not interested in missions, and her own dreams of missionary work faded. That is, until she heard that YWAM was making a way for young people to be missionaries.

"My parents pushed me into coming out to lunch," Darlene explained. "They thought I might be interested in YWAM—and maybe even in you—but that's not what I wanted. I even wore my ugliest dress so you wouldn't be interested in me!"

Loren laughed. *At least that explains the awful dress,* he thought to himself.

"You said something to me that I couldn't ignore," Darlene went on.

"What was that?" Loren asked.

"You told me that not everyone can be a preacher but that every Christian does have a call of his or her own. And that I had to obey that call, no matter how many things came along that tried to derail me." She wiped a tear from her eye. "That night I got down on my knees, and I told God that I would follow Him whatever the cost." Her voice grew soft. "I asked Him to change my desire, and I promised to never marry if that's what He wanted me to do. Guess what happened next?" Her eyes were suddenly shining with excitement.

"I don't know," Loren replied.

"The guy I'd been seeing called me the next morning, and he wanted to know what had happened at 10:30 the night before. I said, 'What do you mean?' And he said, 'I just had this feeling that right at that moment I lost you. What were you doing then? Who were you with?' That was just the time I was praying for God to change my desire. Amazing, isn't it?"

"Yes," Loren said, "but I'm confused about one thing. When you promised to follow God no matter what the cost, did He tell you that He wanted you to stay single, or was that your idea?"

Darlene dropped her head and fell silent.

So that's it! Loren thought. *Darlene thinks she can't marry if she's going to the mission field.*

The conversation continued, and Loren discovered that his hunch was correct. He was relieved to learn this because he liked Darlene a lot. She was lots of fun, and he found that they had many things to talk about. There was much about her that interested him, and she seemed to really care about people, which was important to him.

Loren liked Darlene so much, in fact, that he decided to introduce her to his mother! On their fifth date, Loren picked up Darlene and drove her back to his house. The closer he got to home, the more nervous he became. His mom was not like other Southern California mothers he knew. She had been born in Indian country and raised in a covered wagon in the midst of an outspoken, spirited family. She was known to say exactly what she thought. Loren just hoped she thought good things about Darlene, because if she didn't, she would tell her.

When the young couple reached the door, Loren's parents opened it and stood waiting. Loren's father shook Darlene's hand heartily and welcomed her into the house. Loren's mother, on the other hand, just stood silently sizing up Darlene. Then she reached out and felt Darlene's shoulders and arms. Loren waited to see what his outspoken mom would do next. "You're too bony," he heard his mother say. "And your skirt's too short!"

"I am not, and it is not!" Darlene shot back instantly as she smiled and held out her hand.

Jewell Cunningham stood for a long moment and then threw up her arms and gave Darlene a smothering hug. The two of them started laughing, and Loren let out a sigh of relief. Darlene had the spunk to take his mother in stride. Now that was saying something!

Soon afterward Darlene had to return home and go back to her nursing career, but she and Loren flew to meet each other as often as they could. Even when they were apart, Loren found himself thinking about what a good partner Darlene would be. She loved God, loved adventure, and would not even care where she slept on their missionary travels!

Just before Christmas 1962, Loren became convinced he had found a life partner. As he sat in Blum's restaurant in San Francisco eating cake with Darlene, he decided to ask her to marry him. His heart beat wildly as he began to speak. "Darlene, I'd like to spend the rest of my life with you."

Darlene chatted on, and Loren wondered whether she had heard what he had said, or perhaps she had not caught the meaning of his words. It took him five minutes before he broached the subject again. "I'm serious, Dar. Will you marry me?"

This time there was no mistaking the message. Darlene looked into his eyes. "I'll have to think about it," she said.

Loren's heart dropped, and then he saw her

eyes light up. "Okay, I've thought about it. Yes!" she said.

Loren hardly dared believe what he had just heard. *Yes!* Darlene Scratch was going to be his wife. He imagined their life together in Youth With A Mission. The tiny organization was growing, and Loren knew that things could only get better with Darlene at his side.

Chapter 11

The First Wave

The wedding date was set for June 14, 1963, and Loren had a lot to do before then. He wanted to buy a house, not to live in but as a small nest egg for him and Darlene, and he began looking for a reasonably priced place. He found a four-bedroom home in La Puente that seemed to be a solid investment and scraped up enough money for a small down payment. His father cosigned the mortgage with him, and then Loren rented out the house. Once this was done, Loren turned his attention to the upcoming Youth With A Mission projects.

Although YWAM had sent out twenty vocational volunteers, it was a long way from the waves of young evangelists Loren had in mind. Loren was determined to do something about it. Recalling the great time he had had in the Bahamas with the quartet, he decided to organize a summer outreach there for the summer of 1964. Ideas for the outreach came thick and fast. They would call it a Summer of Service and invite one hundred young people to join them for two months of evangelism and hard work. With enough effort, Loren was convinced that they could reach every home on each of the more than thirty inhabited out islands as well as the Turks and Caicos Islands.

Over Easter, just two months before his wedding, Loren flew to the Bahamas to set up the outreach. The local churches were enthusiastic and offered to help in any way they could. It did not take long before itineraries were settled, transportation arranged, and housing finalized for the team of young people.

Loren planned two other YWAM Summer-of-Service outreaches as well. One was a door-to-door outreach in twelve cities in Utah, and the other involved a team that would go to the Dominican Republic. That would certainly keep everyone busy!

When Loren returned from his planning trip in the Bahamas, wedding plans were in high gear. He was grateful that Darlene and her mother had things well under control, and everything went off without a hitch. Loren grinned for nearly the whole service, for which both his father and Pastor Scratch officiated. Phyllis sang a solo, and Janice lit the candles. But best of all to Loren, Darlene was standing beside him looking stunning in a white silk gown and veil. Loren could not imagine a more perfect wedding, or reception for that matter. Both Aunt Sandra and Aunt Arnette attended the wedding. This was the first whole-family wedding, and everything felt so complete.

The honeymoon mirrored the thing that mattered most to Loren. The couple spent a weekend in Carmel, California, before setting out on a mission trip through Europe and Asia. As they traveled, they went to many of the places Loren had visited on his earlier trips. How good it was this time to have someone to share his insights with.

When they returned to the United States, Loren and Darlene threw themselves into the work of planning the first Summer of Service. They worked out that each person would have to pay $160 for the two-month event. That would include room and board and airfare from Miami to Nassau and back. It was a lot of money for a young person to come up with, but Loren noticed a strange thing as he went from church to church throughout the country recruiting for the event. The tougher he made the requirements, the more enthusiastic the young people became. It was as if they were sitting in their padded pews waiting for someone to offer them a rugged boot-camp experience and the chance to do something life changing with their summer. Each participant had to have his or her parents' written permission and, in most cases, had to have graduated from high school.

Nearly 150 young people from all over the United States signed up for the Summer of Service in the Bahamas. Loren bought three used school buses to make the treks to Florida from Los Angeles and Dallas. Along the way the buses would pick up many of the young people who had signed up to go. As usual, money was short, so Loren and Darlene sold their car to raise their own fees.

On June 24, 1964, one bus left Los Angeles and two left Dallas. The first Summer of Service had begun! By the time they drove through Georgia, there was hardly room to move aboard the buses, which overflowed with sleeping bags, suitcases, and boxes of canned tuna, macaroni and cheese, milk powder, and Spam.

When they arrived in Nassau, Loren received quite a shock. Despite his best efforts at organizing things in advance, the plan was in shambles. One of the key churches that was going to help the YWAM teams had decided that an outreach of young people would not work after all and had withdrawn its support. Other individuals and groups who had promised everything from yachts to tents had either forgotten their commitments or not taken them seriously. It didn't occur to Loren to send everyone home. They had come to evangelize the islands, and he was determined to do it, with or without support. Even if no one else did, Loren believed in the power of young people joining together and reaching out to others.

The teams spent two days regrouping in Nassau, during which time some wonderful things happened. The islands could all be reached by mail boat, and the mail boat owners agreed to let the teams ride on the vessels free of charge. Now the twenty-five teams had a way to get where they were going. Local Christian young people caught the vision as well and teamed up with the American youth to make combined YWAM teams. Each team had a leader, a treasurer, a transportation coordinator, a cook, a reporter/photographer, and a literature leader. There was enough canned food to make do for the remaining six weeks, as well as boxes of books and tracts. The only thing they lacked was accommodations, and Loren challenged the teams to pray and ask God to provide it for them after they arrived on their islands, just like in Luke chapter 10, where Jesus sent out the first short-term teams.

On July 1 the first three teams were waved off from the dock at Nassau. They were headed for Long Island, a thirty-one-hour boat trip away. Other teams quickly followed, until by the end of the week all of the YWAMers were on the various inhabited islands of the Bahamas. Some of the more remote islands had no telephones, and Loren had no way to communicate with the teams except by personal visit.

As soon as the last team was dispatched, Loren and Darlene jumped aboard a small airplane owned and piloted by a local Christian man and started their round of visits to encourage the teams. Sometimes Loren and Darlene were the ones who came away encouraged, as on their trip to Long Island.

A young college student named Jimmy Rogers met them at Long Island. He was brimming over with news.

"You should have been here!" Jimmy started as soon as Loren and Darlene climbed out of the plane. "God has opened so many doors for us here. It started before we even got off the mail boat. We began visiting with the other passengers, and the next thing we know, the mate offers us a car and a house to stay in the first few nights. He even went and got a dump truck in which to take us and our gear back to the house!"

Loren laughed. He had heard of a lot of means of missionary transportation, but a dump truck was a first.

"And we are over halfway through visiting every house on the island," Jimmy continued. "We have a map, and we color in the places we have covered. The island's one hundred miles long and five miles wide, so we sent one of the girls' teams down to the other end, and we are going to meet somewhere in the middle. We give our testimonies to the people we meet, and then we ask them if they want to be saved, and we invite them to a meeting that night."

Jimmy paused to catch his breath. "The Bahamians on the team are fitting right in, and we haven't had any trouble finding places to hold the meetings, either. Word seems to go on ahead of us, and places open up. The girls' team is having a great time too. People are being saved, and one man with a withered arm was healed!"

The next day Loren and Darlene were riding with Jimmy in the car that had been lent to the team. The dump truck, which had come into town to pick up supplies, was a mile or so ahead of them as they headed out to join Jimmy's team.

Just as the car rounded a downhill curve, Loren spotted the dump truck driver, Larry White, standing on the side of the road. The truck was nowhere to be seen.

Jimmy pulled over. "What happened, Larry?" he asked as Loren climbed from the car.

Larry ran his fingers through his hair and then shook his head. "I've never seen anything like it," he replied. "The brakes gave out coming down the hill, and I couldn't make the corner. I went barreling that way." He pointed toward two ruts in the ground. "I was headed straight for a tree when the truck just kind of came to a stop before I hit it, like something was holding it. I got out and looked underneath, and there were vines wound around the axles. Can you believe that? God was watching out for me, that's for sure!"

Loren nodded. He could believe it. He had heard similar stories from other teams. It seemed to him that God really was taking extra special care of these young people. At the next stop Loren told the story of Larry and the dump truck and of the healed man, and he collected new stories to take on to the next teams he visited.

While in the Bahamas, the YWAM teams started two churches, and more than six thousand people expressed an interest in following Christ. Eight years after Loren had seen the moving picture in his mind's eye in Nassau, the first wave of young people was under way. As far as Loren could tell, the teams had met their goal, and every home in the thirty outer islands had been visited.

The teams returned to Nassau for a final evangelistic push. Loren had rented an old air force hangar on the outskirts of the city and transformed it into a small village for the teams to stay in. The building was primitive, with gaps showing between the corrugated iron sheets that formed its shell, but everyone had somewhere to sleep and wash, and a steady flow of good food came from the makeshift kitchen set up on the no longer used tarmac. During the day the teams went door-to-door around Nassau, and in the evenings they held citywide rallies.

The weather, which had been hot but calm, turned wet as a tropical depression neared the islands. Late one evening, just as the teams were returning in flatbed trucks from one of the rallies, streaks of lightning lit up the sky and thunder boomed around them. And then heavy rain began to fall. Everyone laughed and sang in the tropical downpour.

Back at the hangar, however, Loren, who was in charge of everyone's safety, began to get concerned. "You know, Darlene, there's a lot of water pouring in through the gaps in the metal roof. No one seems to mind too much, but I wonder what might happen if the wind starts up."

"Yes, the hangar seems very flimsy to me, too," Darlene agreed.

Loren became even more concerned the next morning, August 22, when he tuned in his radio and heard that Hurricane Cleo was barreling across the Caribbean Sea toward them. He hurried to the local weather bureau and asked to see the chief. "How serious is the threat of Hurricane Cleo to us?" he asked.

The man shook his head. "Let me put it this way, man," he said. "If I had any way to get my family out before it hits, I'd take it. But it's too late—the airport has been closed."

Loren's heart sank. His outreach "family" had more than 140 members. There was no way they could all get spare seats on airplanes back to Miami right now, even if the airport were open. They would just have to trust God and wait it out.

Tension began to build as Loren listened to the radio reports of Hurricane Cleo's progress as it rolled over the Dominican Republic and Haiti and took a curve to the northwest toward the Bahamas. Since Loren knew that the teams could not stay in the hangar, he arranged for them to be evacuated to Evangelistic Temple, a two-story concrete-block structure in town. Loren rested easy once everyone was inside the church. He knew they would all be safe there, and he had received a radio message saying that the team in the Dominican Republic was safe as well.

Hurricane Cleo battered the Bahamas for a day, and when the storm was over, radio reports told a grim story. At least 138 people were dead, hundreds were injured, and thousands were left without homes or livelihoods. Loren and the teams thought back to all of the ramshackle little houses they had visited on the outer islands and wondered which of them were still standing and which inhabitants had not made it through the hurricane.

"We are going home in a few days. I just wish there were something we could do!" Loren confided in Darlene. "We could do so much if we had food, clothing, and building supplies. But we need so much, we'd need a ship to get it all here."

As Loren listened to himself speak, a thought took hold in his mind—a ship filled with young people, all eager to share the gospel and lend a helping hand during crises. As his heart raced, Loren had the strange feeling that this was not an idle thought but another step in fulfilling the "waves of young people" vision. He found himself wondering how long it would be before it would come to pass.

The teams cleaned up the church and shoveled debris from nearby lots until it was time to get on the airplane and head back to the United States. There was not nearly as much chatter on the trip back. Everyone was exhausted, but it was a contented kind of exhaustion. Loren, for his part, could hardly wait to get back and make final plans for the next outreach. He had learned so much, and he wanted to put it into practice.

Chapter 12

Multiplication

For the next two months after they arrived home, Loren and Darlene visited churches telling about the great response the YWAM teams had had and how they were planning bigger outreaches for the coming summer. They went as far south as Dallas, Texas, where the engine of the VW van they were driving blew. It took two days to fix, putting Loren behind schedule to get back to Los Angeles in time to lead a Sunday-morning service.

It was Wednesday before they set out, and Loren was convinced they could make it back in time if he and Darlene took turns driving and sleeping. Sometime early Thursday morning, Loren handed the wheel over to Darlene and settled in the backseat for a nap. He was fast asleep when he was awakened by a huge jolt.

Bam! His head hit against the door handle. The van rolled a quarter turn, and his knees slammed into the roof. Another turn and he was flung halfway out the broken side window. The road came rushing toward him. Instinctively he pushed his hands onto the pavement in front of him and threw his body back inside before he could be crushed between the van and the pavement. Then there was blackness.

When he regained consciousness, Loren found himself lying on the ground. A cloud of dust rose into the air, and through it he could just make out the crumpled outline of a van. He struggled to put the image into context. Where was he? Had he been in the van? If so, where was he going? Why was he now lying in the sand?

As the dust settled, Loren's memories slowly returned. This was his van; the suitcases and clothes strewn around the van were his...and Darlene's. Darlene! Where was she? Loren blinked the blood out of his eyes and struggled to his knees. Then he spotted her, lying facedown in the sand, a suitcase covering her torso. He crawled frantically toward her. A gash running the length of the back of her head revealed her skull. Loren pushed the suitcase off her and rolled her over. Darlene's mouth was set and her eyes were blank. Loren held his cheek very close to her mouth to feel her breath. There was none.

Loren tried to think of what to do, but nothing came to him. He was sitting in the middle of the desert cradling his wife's lifeless body. Suddenly, unexplainably, out of nowhere, Loren heard someone call his name. Somehow he knew it was God's voice. "Yes, Lord," he responded.

"Loren, will you still serve Me?" the voice asked.

Loren looked at Darlene's body.

"Yes, Lord, I'll serve You. I have nothing left except my own life...and You can have that, too," he said as the tears and blood mingled together and flowed down his face.

"Then pray for Darlene," the voice said.

Loren was shocked. He had not even thought of praying for Darlene. After all, she wasn't breathing. What was there to pray for? Nonetheless, Loren obeyed the voice and began to pray that Darlene would recover. He was stunned when he heard a gurgling sound as she began to gasp for breath. Loren kept praying, and Darlene kept drawing breath, even though she was still unconscious.

Within minutes a Mexican man drove by in a pickup truck and surveyed the scene. "I'll go for the police!" he yelled out the window. Loren nodded, and the Good Samaritan sped off.

Loren stayed beside Darlene praying for her to keep breathing. It took the ambulance almost an hour to arrive. As it drove away from the site of the accident, Loren realized why nothing looked familiar to him. While he was sleeping, Darlene must have somehow turned off the main highway and onto a small side road that led to the Mexican border. No wonder there were no other cars on the road.

An hour and fifteen minutes later, the ambulance arrived at the hospital, located ninety miles away from the accident scene. Loren and Darlene were put into adjoining cubicles in the emergency room. Loren had his head bandaged and a back brace fitted. While he was being attended to, his ears were tuned toward the curtain that divided him and his wife. Loren heard the doctor giving instructions for various monitors to be hooked up to Darlene's body. Then he heard a sound he would never forget. It was Darlene frantically calling his name!

"I'm here, honey. It's all right," he called, as fresh tears sprang to his eyes. He had thought he would never hear that voice again.

It was several days before Darlene was well enough to be released from the hospital. She had badly bruised her back and neck, and the gash on the back of her head needed a lot of stitches.

When Darlene was well enough to travel, Loren's father came to pick them up. He told them a story that made Loren's hair stand on end.

"You know, Loren," his father said as they drove along, "at the exact time of your accident, a group of women from a church in Los Angeles were holding a prayer meeting. Even though none of us knew about the accident, one woman felt that they should pray specifically for the two of you. Another woman, a church secretary in Northern California, felt she should spend her lunch break praying for you both. She had been on the Bahamas outreach."

Loren and Darlene were awestruck. At the lowest moment in their lives, God had recruited praying friends hundreds of miles away to help them!

By the beginning of 1965, the accident was behind them and YWAM was running along smoothly. Many young people from the previous Summer of Service were signing up again and encouraging their friends to come as well. Teams went out to Puerto Rico and Central America and into the Pacific islands of Hawaii and Samoa.

The number of young people involved continued to grow steadily. But Loren was still dissatisfied. Somehow all that was happening did not live up to his vision of wave after wave of young people reaching the shores of every continent, at least not yet anyway.

Meanwhile Loren's younger sister Janice married Jimmy Rogers, and in 1965 they began working in New Zealand for Youth With A Mission. They promised to scout out opportunities for a large outreach somewhere in the Pacific islands while they were there.

In January 1967 Loren boarded an airplane for New Zealand. He was alone, since Darlene was staying in Los Angeles to help coordinate the next Summer of Service. Of course January was midsummer in the Southern Hemisphere, and Loren was headed for Great Barrier Island, which lay across the Hauraki Gulf to the east of Auckland, New Zealand's largest city.

During the long flight from Honolulu to Auckland, Loren thought about the future. Two words came to his mind: *addition* and *multiplication*. Right now Youth With A Mission was growing by addition. Loren and Darlene had recruited the six full-time workers with YWAM, as well as many of the young people going out during the summers. They did most of the recruiting work themselves, but what they needed now was multiplication, that is, others who would begin recruiting people for YWAM outreaches, starting various YWAM projects all over the world, without Loren's or Darlene's direct involvement.

That is exactly the problem, Loren thought as he wiggled around to a more comfortable position in the narrow airplane seat, *but how do we solve it, Lord? How do we get to a place where YWAM is taking off in all directions, with able leaders who can direct things in different locations?*

Loren hoped that his time in New Zealand would yield some answers. As he met the enthusiastic mix of young people who were spending their summer vacation at Orama Christian Fellowship on Great Barrier Island, his hopes soared. If he could just find the key to multiplication, Loren was sure that the waves of young people he had seen in his vision would become a reality.

Loren spent a delightful two weeks on the island with Janice and Jim, Neville Winger, the founder and director of the fellowship, and a couple named Jim and Joy Dawson. The 150 young New Zealanders there were amazing. As Loren described his idea about taking an outreach to the Pacific islands, many of them pledged themselves to be a part of it. They were eager to get going, and Jim and Janice had planned just the thing to get them started. Following the two weeks on the island, there was to be a month-long outreach into Ponsonby, one of the suburbs of the sprawling city of Auckland. Jim and Janice had done their homework. Ponsonby had high unemployment and a high concentration of Pacific islanders.

Loren could hardly wait to see how this dynamic group of young people would fare on the outreach. But as he stood on the deck of the ferry taking him from the island back to Auckland, Loren had a strange sense that he should spend the first week of the outreach in prayer and fasting—alone. It was not an easy choice to make, especially since Jim and Janice had been waiting for him to arrive and "take over," but Loren felt strongly that he was to excuse himself from the first week of the Auckland outreach. During that week he stayed in the guestroom at the Dawsons' home in Auckland, praying, fasting, and reading his Bible.

At the end of the week Loren felt refreshed. His time in prayer had left him with much to ponder, but for now it was time to turn his attention to helping with the Ponsonby outreach. Loren felt ready for the challenge, but his heart sank a little when he learned that the one hundred thousand tracts Jim and Janice had ordered for the outreach were all soaking wet. The tracts had been stored in a basement that had flooded. Jim had not bothered Loren with the news during his prayer week, but now Loren joined the small group who were hanging the tracts outside on makeshift clotheslines to dry them.

Then it was time to hit the streets, knocking on doors to share the gospel and hand out the puckered tracts. Loren paired up with an eighteen-year-old Polynesian youth named Kalafi Moala. As they walked from house to house, Kalafi told Loren his life story. He had been born and raised in Tonga, a small island kingdom directly north of New Zealand. A year before, he had been drinking and getting into trouble. One night he came home drunk and suddenly saw that his life was on the fast track to nowhere. Recalling the many sermons he had been obliged to sit through in church, Kalafi called on God and asked Him for a new heart. Kalafi explained that everything had changed after that: many of his school friends had been converted, and the whole atmosphere of his school was changed.

As they walked, Loren became very excited. He sensed that this was just the kind of young leader he was looking for—a leader who could become a part of the multiplication of Youth With A Mission.

Three nights later Loren was sitting at a Christian coffeehouse that YWAM was using to coordinate its outreach. Kalafi grabbed a cup of coffee and plunked himself down next to him. He almost had to yell over the blaring music. "Loren, I think we need a YWAM team to come to Tonga."

Loren nodded and gestured for them to go into the adjoining room, where it was quieter.

"When?" was Loren's first question.

"This July is the coronation of our new king, Taufa'ahua Tupou IV. It will be held in the capital, Nuku'alofa, and they're expecting thousands of Tongans and important people from all over the world to attend."

That was only five months away, and Loren had a busy schedule back in the United States. His heart beat as he posed the next question. "Do you think you could work with Jim and Janice to get the whole thing off the ground?"

Kalafi grinned. "I'll work with you full-time. I've decided to give up the plans I had to make it big in New Zealand and do what I can to set this up."

Loren grinned back. "Okay, let's do it!" Somehow he knew the multiplication had begun.

The two of them prayed for Tonga, and then Loren went off to tell Janice and Jimmy the good news. Not only did they have a focus for their Pacific islands outreach, but also they had a zealous, influential young Tongan man to open doors for YWAM there.

Loren's heart soared as he prepared to return to Hawaii. So many things had clicked while he had been in New Zealand, both during his week of prayer and fasting and during the outreach.

As Loren boarded the airplane and settled in for the long flight to Hawaii, he finally had time to reflect on what he had experienced. With excitement, he recalled a new idea that had come to him during his time of prayer and fasting, a concept he was sure God had revealed to him. It was the idea of a training school, a kind of Christian boot camp where young people could come and learn the ways of God before setting out on an outreach. It would be like the two weeks he had spent on Great Barrier Island, only longer, with the teachers and students all living together, all learning from each other, and all seeking to hear God's direction for their lives.

Loren was excited to think that Darlene would be joining him in Honolulu for a short vacation before they headed back to the mainland together. As Loren thought about his wife, he realized what incredibly privileged childhoods the two of them had enjoyed. Both had grown up in godly homes where it was normal to pray about situations and expect God to answer. Loren thought back to the time when his mother had prayed about the lost five-dollar bill and then they had found it under a bush.

In a very real sense Loren's parents and grandparents were YWAMers to their own generations, but how many other young people had such a rich heritage? Loren could not think of very many. In fact, some of the young people who went on outreaches came from very difficult backgrounds. As Loren sipped a glass of orange juice, he saw that this lack of godly training was one of the reasons there were not more full-time workers with the organization. He believed that this idea of a school might just be the way to change that!

The more Loren thought about it, the more he wondered why he had not thought of a school before. He couldn't wait to share this new idea with Darlene.

Chapter 13

Hotel Golf

It was not until the day after his arrival in Honolulu that Loren felt the time was right to tell Darlene about his new idea. The two of them were sitting on a cliff overlooking the Pacific Ocean. As the waves crashed onto the pitted lava rocks below, Loren explained to Darlene that while he was in New Zealand, he had felt that he should fast and pray for a week.

"That's amazing, Loren!" Darlene responded, her blue eyes sparkling. "I felt led to fast and pray for a week too! Which week were you fasting?"

"Three weeks ago," Loren replied.

"Me too," Darlene said. "What did the Lord tell you?"

"That we should have some kind of school for young people to prepare them to be more effective in missions—and that we're to start it in Switzerland."

Loren watched as tears formed in Darlene's eyes. "Me too," she said, "including Switzerland. Oh, Loren, God is starting to move."

As the two of them sat side by side, ideas began to flow. It would be a school where practical teachers could tell students about God's character and His love for the world, and where the students could learn to hear and follow God's voice. The school could have an outreach phase as well so that the young people could get to know each other in class and then go out in teams to preach and help out in needy countries.

Since they did not know anyone in Switzerland or when the school should be held, Loren and Darlene decided not to tell anyone just yet about their new idea. They would wait until they knew a lot more about it themselves. They did not want to do things just because they seemed like good ideas. They needed to know for sure that even the location was God's idea.

As they waited for plans for the first Youth With A Mission school to unfold, Loren and Darlene had plenty of other things to occupy their minds. The Summer of Service was bigger than ever. One team went off to the World's Fair in Montreal, with the goal of putting a piece of Christian literature in every home in Quebec. Other teams fanned out across North America, and of course, news filtered back from Jim and Janice Rogers about the coronation outreach in Tonga.

International telephone calls were extremely expensive, but the basic information was relayed to Loren in a few quick conversations. Kalafi Moala had exceeded everyone's expectations as an up-and-coming leader. He recruited twenty Tongans to work alongside the thirty-four New Zealanders and Americans who came to evangelize in the island nation. Janice told excitedly how they had given out thousands of tracts and how hundreds of people had responded to the gospel during the ten-day coronation celebration. Some of the teams had gone on to all thirty-three populated islands in Tonga and reached every village with the gospel.

Loren's heart soared as he heard this. It was really working! YWAM was being multiplied in other places without his direct input. He could not wait to see what would happen next.

Loren had not guessed that what would happen next would occur while he was in bed with the flu. It was a chilly fall day as Loren lay on his back, his throat sore and his joints aching. He was not thinking of anything in particular when a thought popped into his head. *Your school in Switzerland is to start in the winter of 1969, and it is to be called a School of Evangelism.*

Loren was still wondering whether this thought had come from God or from his own imagination when a second thought whizzed through his mind. *You are to have visiting teachers.*

Loren wondered whether he was really hearing God's voice. He needed to know for sure. Switzerland still seemed to Loren like a strange place to run a school. Europe was the only continent where Youth With A Mission had no workers or contacts. Workers from the organization had gone out to Africa, Latin America, the Caribbean, the South Pacific, and Asia but not Switzerland.

When he discussed it with Darlene, they decided to make plans to go to Switzerland in the spring to check it out. In the meantime they would ask God to underline whether the instructions were really from Him. Again both of them agreed not to tell anyone else about the school or why they were planning to go to Switzerland until God had confirmed it to them in some clear fashion.

In the midst of all of this, Loren and Darlene began waiting for another event—Darlene was expecting a baby in July 1968.

Two days before Loren and Darlene were set to depart for Switzerland to look for a place to hold the School of Evangelism, Loren's father spoke to him. "Willard Cantelon called me today and asked me to breakfast tomorrow at the Van de Kamp Restaurant in Glendale. He said to be sure to bring you along because it's very important that he talk to you."

Loren was puzzled. Willard Cantelon was a well-known Bible teacher and an old friend of the family. But he had never insisted that Loren go to breakfast with him before. Loren agreed to go, even though he had a thousand details to take care of before he and Darlene set out for Switzerland.

Loren and his father and Willard Cantelon all arrived at the restaurant at the same time and scooted into a vinyl-covered booth. It did not take Willard long to get to the point. As soon as he had ordered sausage and eggs, he said, "Loren, I have a message for you."

Loren sat up and paid attention.

"Last week when I was praying, the Lord spoke to me about you starting a school in Switzerland."

Loren sat listening intently as Willard went on. "God also showed me a few other things. This school will draw students from all over the world, and visiting teachers, too." He looked at Loren and hastily added, "I'm not to be one of the teachers. I'm just a channel to pass this message on to you."

"Thank you," Loren stammered. "God has shown me that, too. In fact, Darlene and I are leaving tomorrow for Switzerland."

Willard smiled. "My message was just God's way of letting you know that you are on track. Do you know anyone in Switzerland?"

"No," Loren replied.

"Well, I do," Willard continued. "He owns a hotel with an annex. Perhaps you can rent part of the hotel and start your school. Let me see... I have his name and address in my book somewhere. He's from somewhere near Lausanne."

With that, Willard Cantelon began leafing through his address book. Meanwhile Loren's mind whirled. What were the odds of someone thinking that YWAM should start a school and run it in Switzerland of all places? *Close to zero,* Loren thought, *unless God was in it!*

As soon as breakfast was over, Loren raced back to tell Darlene the wonderful news. They were on the right track. God *did* want them to go to Switzerland and find a place to hold a School of Evangelism!

Loren and Darlene arrived in Geneva, Switzerland, in April 1968. Willard Cantelon's contact met them at the airport and drove them out to a small village called Chateau d' Ocx, near Lausanne, where they toured a hotel with an annex that Loren felt would be perfect for their first school.

With the arrangements made to rent the facility, Loren and Darlene headed back to the United States. Loren planned to meet with about fifty YWAMers in New York City and Long Island. Then he planned to be back in California in time for the baby's birth. Meanwhile Darlene had gone back to Redwood City, California, to stay with her parents.

Loren had just crossed the Hudson River in New York on July 3, 1968, when he decided to stop and call Darlene.

"How would you like to be a father before today is over?" she asked.

"But that day's three weeks away," Loren replied.

"Not according to the baby," said Darlene. "The doctor is sure it's on its way."

"I'll be there if I can," Loren said. It was the worst possible day of the year for last-minute traveling, but he managed to get a flight to California and arrived at the hospital just after midnight. He was just in time for his baby daughter, Karen Joy, to make her entrance into the world. The child was blue-eyed and blonde, just like her mother. In no time at all she was cooing and smiling, and Loren and Darlene were grateful to have such a happy, contented baby.

After Karen's birth, Darlene was able to continue her work alongside Loren as they supervised the growing number of outreaches around the world and planned the upcoming School of Evangelism in Switzerland. As they had done with the name Youth With A Mission, they soon shortened School of Evangelism to the initials SOE.

In January 1969, Loren and Darlene, along with Karen, headed back to Lausanne, Switzerland. After three months in the classroom, the twenty-eight students who had been attending the school headed out on an outreach with Loren and Darlene and baby Karen. They visited twelve nations, including several behind the Iron Curtain in Communist Eastern Europe, where they shared the gospel.

While they were away, the lease expired on the original facility, and Loren and Darlene were left scrambling to find somewhere to hold the next School of Evangelism, which had already been advertised. Many young people had inquired about attending. Loren and Darlene prayed fervently that God would help them find a suitable place, and soon!

One morning in early August 1969, Loren learned of a hotel on the outskirts of Lausanne. He was told that it was old and run-down, but it was big. And space was something Loren needed. He was thinking big, perhaps up to a hundred students attending the school.

That afternoon Loren and Darlene, with Karen in her stroller, walked out to see the hotel. It was quite an imposing sight, all five stories of it, set into the side of a hill. Behind it was a forest of fir trees, and in front, a long, sloping lawn. The hotel looked out over green pastures, with the Alps as a backdrop.

"It's a beautiful setting," Darlene said, bending down to unbuckle Karen from her stroller so she could toddle around on the lawn.

Loren spotted faded painted letters on the steep roof. "Look, it's called the Hotel Golf. It's pretty run-down, though. Looks like it's been boarded up for years."

"Yes," Darlene replied. "It must have been some place in its heyday. I wonder how many rooms it has."

"Let's find someone and ask," Loren said as he scooped Karen up and headed for the two-story building next door. "Maybe someone here can tell us a bit more about it."

At the house they found the owner of the hotel. The woman spoke English and explained that since her husband left her, she had been reluctant to rent the hotel. It had been empty for several years. "It has thirty-two rooms, you know, and a large, usable attic. But who can take care of thirty-two rooms these days?" the woman sighed.

"We might be interested. Could we take a look inside?" Loren asked.

"Be my guest," the owner replied, pulling a jangling ring of keys from her pocket. "Here, this one should unlock the front door. Give it a good shove, though. It's been a long time since anyone used that entrance."

Loren took the key, and he and Darlene and Karen headed back toward the hotel. As he turned the key and opened the door, Loren stepped into a time capsule. Cobwebs assailed him from every direction, and he left the door open to provide some light. He peered around the lobby. It had obviously been a regal place once, with its Persian carpets, brocade-and-mahogany chairs, and large gilt-edged mirrors that were all covered in a thick layer of dust.

Darlene flung open a set of French doors that led into what had once been a fine dining room. Chandeliers hung from the ceiling, and a pile of linen napkins still sat on an ornately carved sideboard.

They walked through the room, leaving footprints in the dust, and on up the broad staircase to the rooms.

Loren was a little concerned about what Darlene might think of the place. Was it too bad to consider fixing up for a school due to start in just a few days? Gingerly he broached the subject. "So, do you think we could make this home for a while?" he asked.

Darlene's shining eyes gave him his answer before she even opened her mouth to speak. "Oh, yes! I think it would be great. And with thirty-two rooms, think of all the young people we could train and send out around the world!" she said excitedly.

They explored the rest of the hotel and ended up back in the dining room. "I have a good feeling about this place," Loren said. "Let's pray and ask God to direct our steps as we talk to the owner again."

Loren reached out and hugged Darlene and Karen. "Lord, direct our thoughts. We want them to be Your thoughts. Please show us clearly if we are to rent this place, or if You have somewhere else for us to hold the SOE. In Jesus' name, amen," he prayed.

"Amen!" Darlene seconded as Karen began to squirm.

Just then the owner appeared at the door. "So what do you think?" she asked. "Of course, there is a lot of cleaning up to do, and I cannot do it myself. I have decided to rent it to you if you will clean it yourselves."

"We are interested," Loren replied. "How much would you be asking for the rent?"

The owner gave Loren a very low estimate, which Loren agreed to pay.

"I just feel really good about this!" Loren told Darlene as they walked back down the shaded pathway. "I believe God is going to multiply this training center and make it the first of many."

"I hope so," Darlene replied enthusiastically. "There are so many needs out there, we could do with a hundred places like this!"

Loren chuckled. *Thank You, God, for giving me a wife who can match me vision for vision,* he thought.

A core group of young YWAMers were soon spending their days scrubbing out the Hotel Golf in preparation for the School of Evangelism. Among them were Don and Deyon Stephens from Colorado. Don and Deyon had been on the original Summer of Service outreach in the Bahamas. As they worked, the YWAMers prayed that God would touch the lives of all the young people who passed through the training school and that through their lives, in turn, He would touch the world.

Meanwhile phase one of the School of Evangelism was already under way. This consisted of outreaches and language training in various cities around Europe. Loren kept in touch with the students by phone and mail, and he was thrilled to hear that some of them were already preaching in their newly acquired languages.

By August 15, 1969, the hotel had been thoroughly cleaned, the kitchen renovated, and the attic cleared out. Everything was as ready as it could be for the thirty-six students who were arriving the next day.

Chapter 14

A Growing Mission

Soon the hotel was filled with excited young men in bell-bottom jeans and young women with long, braided hair and wearing flowing dresses. Several of them were graduates of Bible colleges, while others had decided to do the School of Evangelism before or in place of more academic training. The SOE, which was to be fourteen months long in all, called for the students to spend three and a half months in language training. They would spend three months in a lecture phase listening to Loren and other Christian leaders speak on a range of topics, from understanding the New Testament to how to evangelize effectively. Having so many enthusiastic young people gathered together in one place energized Loren.

In April the students set out for a three-month field trip to the Middle East to put what they had learned about evangelism and discipleship into practice. They dispersed among groups of Communists, Jews, and Muslims to explore positive ways in which to present the gospel to them. Following this, they all gathered at the Sea of Galilee, where they camped for two weeks. Loren's father, whom everyone called Uncle Tom, flew in to teach the students while they were camped.

When the students arrived back at the Hotel Golf, they were given another round of teaching, and finally it was time to get ready for the main outreach.

Loren unrolled on the floor a large, laminated map of the world, and everyone gathered around it. As they looked at all the continents and islands of the world, Loren challenged each student to ask God where he or she should go on outreach and whether he or she should stay longer in that place to set up a YWAM base. Soon excited young people confided in Loren that God had called them to France, Spain, Germany, England, Holland, and Denmark.

In addition, Janice and Jimmy, who had just joined the group, felt led to attempt to get the gospel into Afghanistan. Jimmy made some inquiries and was soon offered sixteen thousand Gospels of John in the Farsi language, one of the main languages of Afghanistan. It was risky taking Christian literature into a fundamentalist Muslim country, but as Janice and Jim and the students who were going to accompany them prayed about the situation, they felt confident that this was what God wanted them to do.

Soon all of the suitcases and backpacks were hauled down from the hotel attic, and everyone was ready to head off on the outreach.

Loren, accompanied by Darlene, who was now expecting their second child, spent the three months of the outreach visiting the various teams at work. Loren could hardly wait until the end of the outreach, when everyone would get to tell the stories he was hearing as he went from team to team. However, it was the team in Afghanistan, which he did not visit, who had the most exciting story of all.

At the end of the outreach everyone gathered again at Hotel Golf. Jimmy and Janice and their team drove all the way back from Afghanistan to Lausanne. When their van finally pulled up to the hotel, Janice leaped out, rushed up to Loren, and gave him a big hug. "Oh, Loren, you'll never guess what an amazing time we've had!" she exclaimed.

"Tell me!" Loren replied, gathering several other YWAMers around him so they could listen too.

"Things were going well, right up to the time we were arrested! The whole team was arrested for smuggling Christian literature into the country, and we were scheduled to appear the next day before a group of judges, who were also the religious leaders of the province of Herat. But when we were taken before them, the judges declared that they had read the Gospel of John and liked it! They said we could go free!"

"Great!" Loren exclaimed.

"But that's not all," Janice continued. "We asked them what was going to happen to our literature, and their leader said, 'It's yours, you can take it.' And then, get this, we said, 'What can we do with it?' and he said...go on guess what he said."

Loren laughed. "You're telling the story, sis!"

"He said, 'I suppose if you brought it to give to the Afghani people, then that's what you should do with it!' Can you believe that!"

Loren found himself laughing again. It was such a crazy ending to the smuggling and the arrest that he was sure God had changed the hearts of the judges. Finally he replied, "I've never heard of Afghan officials doing anything like that. What a miracle!"

As the other groups came back, they, too, had great adventures to relate. Many of the students were prepared to go back to the areas they had been in and set up permanent YWAM bases.

Don and Deyon Stephens talked to Loren about a big plan. Don explained that he believed that Youth With A Mission should have a presence at the Munich Olympic Games, which would be held in less than two years' time in the summer of 1972.

Immediately Loren's mind began to buzz with possibilities. The small team who had gone behind the Iron Curtain on the outreach had needed to be so careful not to antagonize the Communist governments. But at the Olympic Games there would be young athletes from many Communist countries who would be free to listen to the gospel, many of them for the first time.

"There'll be lots of challenges ahead," Loren told Don. "How many YWAMers do you think God wants at the games?"

Don hesitated for a moment, and then he said quietly, "I was thinking around two hundred."

Loren nodded. "I guess you'd better get started on the planning. You have less than two years!" he added with a grin.

Here it was again: YWAMers were beginning to multiply themselves without direct input from Loren, who could not have been happier.

Meanwhile, Loren, Darlene, and a small group of people stayed behind in Switzerland to set about organizing the next School of Evangelism, which they planned to hold again in the Hotel Golf. Darlene helped where she could, but her hands were now full looking after two-and-a-half-year-old Karen and a new baby, David Loren Cunningham, who was born February 24, 1971.

As they prayed about the upcoming school, Loren and Darlene both became convinced that God was telling them to buy the hotel rather than continue renting it. It was a huge step to take. Youth With A Mission had never owned any property before. In fact, Loren and Darlene had never even lived in their own home. They had always stayed with Loren's parents or with Christian families on their recruiting tours. The only property they did own was the house in La Puente that Loren had bought as a nest egg before they were married. Now as they prayed, they felt that God was asking them to sell that house and use the proceeds to help buy Hotel Golf, which had an asking price of 600,000 francs. Loren did a quick calculation in his head: that was about 150,000 U.S. dollars. Once they were convinced that this was God's idea and not their own, Loren sent word back to his sister Phyllis asking her and her husband, Len, to prepare the house for sale.

The day arrived when money was due for the hotel purchase, and they were still ten thousand dollars short. All the YWAM staff at the Hotel Golf prayed extra hard. Loren had no idea where the additional money would come from, since everyone at the hotel had turned his or her pockets inside out to get the fund to its current level. The situation was desperate. If they failed to come up with ten thousand dollars by five o'clock, not only did they lose the hotel but they also lost the ten-thousand-dollar deposit they had already put down. Loren thought about calling his father, but there was nothing practical his father could do. Even if by some miracle he did have a way to get ten thousand dollars in cash, there was no way to get it wired to Switzerland in time to meet the deadline.

On his way to town to meet with the owner and her lawyer, Loren stopped at the post office one last time. Several envelopes were in the box, and as he ripped them open, checks and money orders floated out. There were five of them, and when Loren tallied them, they came to exactly ten thousand dollars and sixty cents—just what they needed to make the payment on the hotel! Loren could hardly wait to get back to the hotel to tell the others how God had provided the money at the very last minute. Everyone was overjoyed by the news.

As the year went by, other Youth With A Mission centers, or bases, as they were called, began to spring up. By Christmas 1971 there were twenty bases, three of them holding their own schools of evangelism, following the model of the original school in Lausanne.

In early 1972 Loren headed to Munich, Germany, with Don Stephens to plan for the Olympic Games outreach that was now just six months away. Somehow Loren felt that he should be prepared for something quite unexpected to happen.

Gary Stephens, Don's brother, had called the week before to say that he had found a solution to the accommodation problem facing the outreach. YWAM had bought a two-ton Heidelberg printing press with which it planned to print a million pieces of literature in English, German, and French to distribute to the athletes and spectators at the games, but so far there was nowhere to put the press. Most of the available space in Munich had been grabbed up at least a year before, and the little that was still available cost a fortune to rent.

The printing press was not the worst of it. Don, Lynn Green, Loren, and Brother Andrew, the founder of Open Doors, a ministry to the persecuted church known for smuggling Bibles behind the Iron Curtain, had traveled throughout the United States, Canada, South Africa, Asia, Australia, New Zealand, and Europe promoting the outreach. As a result, one thousand young Christians had pledged to converge on the Munich Olympic Games! It would be a great outreach if YWAM could just find somewhere to house everyone. So Loren was very interested when Gary called to say that he and another YWAMer, Doug Sparks, had found a solution: a castle! The idea sounded a little preposterous at first, but the more Loren prayed about it, the more convinced he became that YWAM should use the castle not just as housing for the outreach but also as a permanent base in Germany.

When Loren arrived in Munich, Gary was excited to tell him more about the castle. "I can't wait for you to see it, Loren. It's plenty big enough for the printing press and the kids!"

Loren laughed, still amazed at this extravagant solution.

Soon Loren, Brother Andrew, Don, Gary, and Doug were driving toward the small village of Hurlach. "The village has only one thousand residents," Don said cheerfully. "Just think, if we take the castle, we will double the population."

Loren looked out at the flat, orderly landscape dotted with dairy cows and plowed fields. Suddenly a huge castle loomed ahead of them. Loren guessed it was six stories high. With beige stone walls and four round turrets, it looked like something right out of a fairy tale.

"Pretty big, isn't it?" Don laughed.

Loren nodded. "It's huge."

The gates were open, and Don guided the car through them and drove up the circular driveway, stopping at the massive front door.

"The outside looks in great condition," Loren commented. "Not run-down at all."

"That's the beauty of this place," Gary said. "It was built in the sixteenth century, and various attempts have been made over the years to modernize it. The present owners recently upgraded everything: the plumbing, heating, lighting, insulation, floors...everything."

"Why?" Loren asked. "What did they use it for?"

"It was a home for needy kids, but they've moved in closer to Munich," Gary explained as he rang the bell to the left of the ornately carved door. "The amazing thing is that they put twice the asking price into the renovations alone."

A caretaker soon appeared at the door and showed them through the building. Loren got goose bumps. The castle would make a perfect base. There were so many rooms from the attic to the dungeon that it would take weeks to catalog them all. And from the top turret Loren looked out over the castle's two acres of immaculately kept grounds.

"It shouldn't be any trouble housing everyone in here," Don said. Then, pointing down to his left, he added, "Over there I thought we could pitch a big circus tent, where we could have meetings. What do you think of half the kids going into town one day to witness and do dramas and skits while the other half stay here to pray, read the Bible, and listen to Christian teaching in the tent? They could change places the next day, and that way, no one will get too exhausted with the travel and they'll all have the chance to get their spiritual batteries recharged."

"It sounds good to me," Loren replied, glad that Don was turning out to be such an able leader.

The castle seemed perfect for the event, and the next day Loren made an offer to buy it. The seller accepted, and some European friends of YWAM paid the deposit on it. The keys were handed over, and the printing press was delivered and set up.

It was a busy time, although everything was well under control when Loren departed on a pre-arranged trip around the Pacific Rim to visit newly established YWAM bases. Loren was on his way to Hong Kong when he had the strangest idea that now was the right time to pursue buying a ship. He was astonished. He wondered what owning a ship would involve: a crew, home port, insurance, engine maintenance, docking fees, fuel. Owning a hotel and a castle had been challenging, but owning a ship was much more involved. Loren continued to pray about the idea as he circled the Pacific Rim and traveled back to Munich in time for the Olympic Games.

By the time Loren arrived back in Hurlach, young people from all over the world were converging on the castle. Loren was impressed at how focused they were on the task ahead. Most of them had never been to Germany before, yet they gladly exchanged sightseeing for prayer circles and logistical meetings.

On the first day of the Olympic Games, excitement ran high as the first batch of five hundred young evangelists collected their brown-bag lunches at 5 A.M. and headed for the train for the forty-minute trip into Munich. They would not be back until midnight. The five hundred young people who remained at the castle prayed for the outreach and listened to Christian teaching by Brother Andrew, Joy Dawson, Corrie ten Boom, Loren, and others.

As the days went on, the groups became discouraged. Officials in Munich were stalling on writing a permit for the big march that Youth With A Mission hoped to hold on the last day of the games. More discouraging was the fact that it was not easy trying to discuss something as serious as the state of a person's soul in such a festive atmosphere. A few people, particularly those from behind the Iron Curtain, were interested in the gospel, but many others laughed at the young evangelists and told them to get into the party mood. However, fourteen days into the Olympic Games, something happened that stopped the "party" in its tracks.

Early on the morning of Tuesday, September 5, Loren was in the tent speaking to the five hundred young people whose turn it was to stay behind at the castle in Hurlach. As he spoke, he noticed a few people with shocked looks on their faces whispering at the back. Soon someone slipped up to Loren and handed him a note that read, "Terrorists have broken into the Israeli quarters in the Olympic Village. Two of the Jewish athletes are dead, and nine have been taken hostage."

Loren read the note a second time. It was hard to take in. The Olympic Games, the symbol of worldwide brotherhood and sportsmanship, had been hijacked by violence! Loren read the note aloud to the group, and then everyone broke into small groups to pray for the hostages and the terrible situation they were in. By the time the terrorist attack ended in a bloody shootout with German police at the Munich airport, nine more Israelis, one German police officer, and five of the eight Palestinian terrorists were dead.

The following day Loren and Darlene led a team into Munich. How different it was from the previous times they had been there. The festive banners still waved all over town, but the mood was somber. Everywhere Loren looked, he saw stunned people, and as he listened, he heard the same question over and over: "How could this happen?"

No one was telling the YWAM evangelists to get into the party spirit now. In fact, many of the YWAMers found themselves weeping and praying with bewildered athletes and spectators. Now the door was wide open for spiritual conversation.

The Munich officials hurried through the permit for the march to be held right away, and a European Christian couple even donated thousands of cut flowers to give out along the route. The Heidelberg press churned out ten thousand newspapers featuring stories of reconciliation. The photo on the front page showed two YWAMers, one Jewish and one Arab, standing arm in arm proclaiming that Jesus Christ was the only answer to the problems in the world.

At the march, Loren and Don led the way, with over a thousand people gathered behind them. As they marched, they prayed that God would bring hope to hopeless hearts. The response was overwhelming. The crowd that had once been apathetic to the gospel message now grabbed the newspapers and read them on the spot. For the rest of the week, as the Olympic Games continued, Loren and the other YWAMers faced a constant stream of people who wanted prayer and counsel.

When the outreach was finally over, many of the young people who had been involved were so excited about what they had learned and put into practice that they wanted to attend a School of Evangelism and go into full-time mission work. As Loren watched the young people take down the circus tent that had served as their meeting hall, he was convinced that he was looking at many future leaders of Youth With A Mission.

Loren felt satisfied as he and Darlene left Hurlach to return to Lausanne. Enough money had been donated to make the payment on the castle, and a group of young people were eager to stay and set up a permanent base there. They planned to use the printing press to pump out much-needed Christian literature in the French and German languages as well as in Russian and Eastern European languages for the Iron Curtain countries. An important literature ministry was born.

With the Olympics behind him, Loren's thoughts once again turned to the idea of a ship. The vessel would need to be sturdy, with ample cargo space to hold emergency supplies to help out in natural disasters and enough cabin space so that it could be used as a floating School of Evangelism. Loren and Darlene continued to pray, believing that the right ship would come along.

In March 1973, Loren heard about a sturdy inter-island ferry in New Zealand that was up for sale. It was called the *Maori,* after the native people of those islands. It sounded like just the right ship for Youth With A Mission. The following month Loren left Darlene and the two children in Lausanne and flew down to New Zealand to inspect the vessel. The *Maori* was everything Loren hoped it would be, and soon Wally Wenge, a Youth With A Mission worker and a good businessman, was negotiating for its purchase.

Everything went perfectly. Money was donated for the $72,000 deposit, and people with nautical experience volunteered for crew positions. Soon Wally had rallied 110 volunteers and crew members from ten countries to clean the ship, prepare it for a repaint, and make it shipshape for its new life as a missionary ship. Loren was delighted that YWAM would be adding a ship to the hotel and castle that it now owned.

As things progressed with the ship, Loren flew to Osaka, Japan, to attend a Youth With A Mission meeting of about one hundred leaders from around the world. They were going to pray and make plans for the future of the fast-growing mission.

On his way to Osaka, Loren made a stopover in Seoul, Korea. One morning as he lay on his bed praying, he had a similar experience to the one in the Bahamas seventeen years before. In his mind he saw a vivid picture in which everyone was cheering for the *Maori* but Jesus was in the shadows. No one was giving thanks to God for providing the vessel. In the picture it was as if Loren and the other YWAMers thought that they could make it all happen with their own power. Deep in the pit of his stomach Loren felt ill. He recognized that feeling—it was pride. And he knew it had taken root in his heart. Right there and then he asked God to forgive him for thinking he could make things happen all by himself.

As Loren flew on to Osaka, the original excitement he felt about the meeting was now replaced with a sense of dread. Instead of celebrating the purchase of the ship and planning for the future, he was going to have to challenge the gathered YWAMers on their pride. And as Loren had done, when the group heard of his experience in Seoul, they, too, asked God to forgive them for their pride.

Although Loren felt sure that God had heard their prayers, he was not surprised when everything started to go wrong with the *Maori*. A businessman who had promised to pay the balance of the asking price suddenly disappeared from view, and although the Union Steamship Company that owned the ship extended the deadline for payment, no more donations came in. It was as if God had sucked the life out of the entire project. Eventually the last deadline passed, and Loren and the other leaders had to give up their dream, losing their deposit and seeing the sturdy little ship sent off to the junkyard.

Some more money, $130,000 in fact, had been donated to purchase the *Maori*. As Loren and his leadership team prayed about what to do with it, they felt that the money should still go toward a ship. Another ministry, named Operation Mobilisation, was in the process of buying a ship to deliver Christian literature around the world. Loren gladly withdrew from the bank the entire amount they had collected to buy the *Maori* and sent it off to help buy the new ship for Operation Mobilisation.

It was a heavy lesson for Loren to learn but one he would never forget. He prayed that sometime in the future God would bless them with another ship, and he promised to acknowledge that it would be a tool to bring glory to God and not to put another notch in YWAM's belt.

Loren was now facing another challenge. At the time when everything was going so well with the *Maori,* Loren had announced that a School of Evangelism would be held onboard the vessel. Ninety students had signed up for the school, and now they had nowhere to go. Loren did not know what to do with them. But as he prayed about the situation, he felt that Youth With A Mission should rent a camp in Hawaii and hold the school there, that is, if anyone still wanted to come.

Amazingly, all ninety of the students adjusted their plans, and Loren, Darlene, and the children met them at a YWCA camp in Kaneohe on the wet side of the island of Oahu. The young people were enthusiastic and ready to learn, which was quite a contrast to how Loren felt. He was exhausted after the drawn-out drama of the ship, and he felt hesitant to step out and lead again. However, the ten weeks at Kaneohe revealed some pieces of the puzzle that would lead Youth With A Mission into new territory.

Chapter 15

Only the Beginning

Three weeks into the School of Evangelism Loren was still smarting from the loss of the *Maori* and decided to hold an all-night prayer meeting with some of the staff. The night started off slowly, but by morning Loren and those who had prayed with him were convinced of three things. First, God wanted them to have a different kind of school, located at Kona on the Big Island of Hawaii. Second, a farm was involved with the school. Third, God was going to replace the *Maori* with another, larger, white ship. This time, though, Loren did not expect all of this to happen at once. He continued on with the School of Evangelism and waited for God to show him—very clearly—the next step.

When the classroom part of the school was over and the students left on their outreach to the Pacific islands, Loren and his family headed back to Switzerland. It was a long trip, and they were glad to see their many old friends again. Don Stephens had been running the base in Lausanne while they were away. Everything had gone very smoothly, so smoothly, in fact, that Loren and Darlene began to wonder whether they were really needed there anymore. As they prayed about it, they both became convinced that their time in Europe was over for now.

New YWAM bases with mobile outreach teams were springing up around Europe, and it was time for Loren and Darlene to turn their attention to the Pacific and Asia. Their hearts beat fast as they prayed about spearheading a new base on the Big Island of Hawaii. Loren saw Hawaii as the crossroads of the Pacific. If they could motivate hundreds of young people of Kalafi Moala's caliber, all sorts of new opportunities could be opened up in Asia.

Not long after Loren and Darlene arrived in Kona, a stranger offered to give Youth With A Mission sixty acres of sloping farmland. YWAM now also owned a large white house, dubbed King's Mansion. Before the year was out, a new style of school was being held there. Loren called it a Discipleship Training School (DTS). It was designed to come before the School of Evangelism and would cover a core curriculum of basic Christian discipleship wherever it was held.

By January 1978 the Cunninghams had been living in Hawaii for over three years. Two hundred fifty staff and students were now there with them, learning about evangelism and preparing outreaches that spanned the globe. During this time, Loren had become interested in the Pacific Empress Hotel. The hotel had forty-five acres, one hundred rooms, a nine-hole golf course, and a swimming pool. It was beautifully situated on the slope of a mountain overlooking Kona Bay. However, it had been in bankruptcy proceedings for the past eight years, and its former splendor had given way to termites and overgrown tropical vines. Drug addicts and homeless people squatted in the rooms, and each year the hotel became more run-down.

Still, whenever Loren drove past the hotel, he felt it had a sense of destiny. He wondered if God might want to use it for the university that Youth With A Mission had planned. The Pacific and Asia Christian University, as Loren hoped to call it, was not a normal university. It would offer a mix of theory and practical application in a number of areas, from health care to biblical counseling to agriculture.

Finally in 1977 Loren had received word that the hotel was going to be sold. Several large property companies wanted to buy it, but as Loren prayed, he felt strongly that the Pacific Empress Hotel was going to become the YWAM university.

When he announced that the hotel was up for sale, the YWAMers in Hawaii took up an offering and raised fifty thousand dollars, not for the hotel but to give away to another needy ministry. They were learning that generosity was God's way to release His promises.

Within days of the YWAMers' offering, Loren received amazing news. Another Christian ministry, named Daystar, wanted to give Youth With A Mission a very large piece of commercial real estate located in Minneapolis/St. Paul, Minnesota. The property was worth a lot of money and could be used as security for a loan to buy the Pacific Empress Hotel. The transaction went smoothly, and soon Loren found himself in court offering to buy the hotel for the amount he believed God had told him to offer—one-fourth the asking price! Much to many people's amazement, the bankruptcy judge accepted the offer, and Youth With A Mission had a facility to use as a university campus.

Thousands of hours of hard work lay between the vision of the university and its reality. Eight years of neglect and trespassers had left the hotel reeking and overrun with tropical plants, cockroaches, rats and centipedes. Still, true to form, the young YWAMers were energetic and optimistic. Eight-year-old Karen and six-year-old David enthusiastically joined in the effort. One by one the hotel rooms and facilities were transformed into habitable units.

Loren and Darlene were among the first people to move onto the property, using three adjoining rooms on the third floor. There was not room for much furniture or other possessions, but that did not matter, since they owned very little. When they moved from country to country, Loren and Darlene had kept their belongings to the baggage allowance on the aircraft.

A week after they moved in, while Loren's back was still sore from wielding a machete day after day as he hacked back the tropical foliage, a man named Dr. Howard Malmstadt came to visit him. Loren had been at a conference with Dr. Malmstadt, a prominent professor and scientist at the University of Illinois. As they sat in an empty room on the third floor looking out over the grounds of the old hotel, Loren told Howard that he believed that God wanted Youth With A Mission to transform the hotel into a university.

"I know," Howard said. "God has already told me about it."

Loren smiled. "Tell me what you mean."

"Well," Howard began, leaning back on the folding canvas chair. "About six months ago I was asked to submit my name for the presidency of a large American university, but I just couldn't feel any peace about the move. So I prayed about it, and I felt strongly that God said, 'I am going to give YWAM a university in Hawaii, and I want you to play a role in it.'"

Loren sat silently for a long moment before he spoke. How grateful he was that God was sending along the professor to guide the birth of such a different ministry.

Within months Howard was living on the "campus." He, Loren, Darlene, and other leaders had regular prayer meetings as they plotted out the future of the Pacific and Asia Christian University in Kona, Hawaii.

It was a good thing that Howard came when he did, because Loren's attention had turned to another matter—a ship. This time it was not a ferryboat but an aged eleven-thousand-ton ocean liner named the *Victoria*. The vessel was long past its prime and waiting to be sold in Venice, Italy. Don Stephens was enthusiastic about the possibility of its belonging to YWAM, but when Loren thought about it, he could not help but recall the debacle over the *Maori*. Still, he agreed to pray about it and urged Don to continue investigating the opportunity. Slowly, over time, Loren came to believe that this was indeed the ship God had for them. One thing that convinced him was another visitor, this time a man from Toronto named Paul Ainsworth. Loren had never met the man before when Paul turned up at the door in Kona.

Paul introduced himself in a strong Canadian accent and asked rather sheepishly if he could speak to Loren. Loren readily agreed and took him down to the freshly painted office on the first floor. It was there that Paul poured out an amazing story that left Loren with goose bumps. Paul told how he'd had the strangest experience, something quite out of the ordinary. He'd seen a vision of a ship sailing around a map of the Pacific Ocean. The vision was so clear, he said, that he could read the names of the islands that the ship passed by, and wherever the ship went, it stirred up revival, causing thousands of Pacific islanders to come to Jesus and become evangelists themselves in Asia.

When the vision ended, Paul did not know what to do next, until God told him to go to Hawaii. Although Paul didn't know a single person in Hawaii, he obediently made travel plans. Just as he was about to leave, a friend handed him a piece of paper with a single name written on it—Loren Cunningham. "That man may be able to help you once you get there. He lives somewhere in Hawaii. I'm not sure where, though, and he travels a lot," his friend had said. With the piece of paper in his pocket, Paul set out and eventually found someone who knew Loren and was able to direct him to Kona.

Tears welled in Loren's eyes as he listened to Paul. How extraordinary, he marveled, that God should send someone all the way from Toronto just to confirm that it was right to go ahead with the ship because it would be such a blessing to so many people.

For his part, Paul seemed relieved that the whole vision made sense to Loren! Now, he confided, he was sure that he had delivered the message to the right person and could go home again secure in that knowledge.

In April 1978 Loren felt it was time to go to Venice and see the ship for himself. He soon found that Don had been very accurate in his description of it. The vessel was a hunk of rusting metal! Everything on it was filthy and seemed to need replacing or refurbishing. The emergency generators did not work, and so as dusk settled, Loren and Don had to disembark the gloomy hulk.

Loren thought back to the Pacific Empress Hotel. At the time it had seemed like a colossal project, but it was nothing compared to an aging ocean liner. The rust would have to be chipped off the vessel, and then the ship would have to go into dry dock to be surveyed and repainted. The engines and generators would have to be overhauled. The list of things that needed to be done went on and on.

Still, the ship had an air of optimism about it, and Loren could not deny the amazing visit only weeks before by Paul Ainsworth. Perhaps, Loren was convinced, this was the ship they were supposed to have. Other ministries soon heard about the ship project, and donations flowed in. Indeed, many substantial donations came from other large ministries, including Last Days Ministries, 700 Club, Billy Graham Evangelistic Association, and David Wilkerson Youth Crusades.

Months of negotiations followed, but eventually Don called Loren to tell him the good news. The contracts had been signed; the ship now belonged to Youth With A Mission. Don even had a name for the vessel: *Anastasis*. Loren heartily agreed. The word was Greek for resurrection, and it fit perfectly.

Loren and Darlene continued to pray and support Don and his team of workers as they began the enormous task of cleaning, painting, and renovating the ship in preparation for service.

In the meantime, the university was progressing. Howard Malmstadt and his wife had moved onto the property, and a well-known architect and campus designer from Illinois had volunteered to create plans for a campus designed around Loren's concept of the seven spheres of influence. The concept had come to Loren while he was praying about how to influence entire nations with the gospel. He came up with seven areas that influence any culture: (1) the family; (2) the church; (3) the schools; (4) the government; (5) the media; (6) arts, entertainment, and sports; and (7) commerce, science, and technology. Loren urged the students he met to use these specific areas to pray for nations and to look for ways to work within them and influence them. The architect designed buildings that reflected these seven spheres and a campus of "villages" symbolizing the world that needed transformation.

As Loren looked over the plans for the new campus, John Dawson, the twenty-seven-year-old son of Jim and Joy Dawson, showed him a *Time* magazine article titled "Doesn't Anybody Care?" The article was about the terrible situation that people fleeing Vietnam and Cambodia found themselves in. Many of these people exchanged everything they owned for passage on leaky boats that often sank once they got out into the ocean, or the people were herded together into grossly overcrowded refugee camps.

"I can't get away from the title 'Doesn't Anybody Care?'" John told Loren. "That's a question I think God is putting to YWAM."

Although Loren had two major projects on his hands that stretched Youth With A Mission far beyond its available resources, he found that he could not get the title out of his head either. Before long he felt he had to go and see the situation for himself. A small party, including Joy Dawson and Loren's assistant, Gary Stephens, set out for Asia.

The first place Loren and his team visited was Camp Jubilee in Hong Kong. Loren had never seen a place less appropriately named; there was nothing at all to celebrate there. Eight thousand Vietnamese refugees were crowded into quarters that were designed to hold nine hundred people. The sewage lines had broken, and eight inches of human waste covered the bottom floor of the sprawling building. The smell was almost too much to endure, and Loren shook his head as he saw entire families wading through the sludge to collect their meager rice rations.

By the end of the tour, Loren and those with him had tears in their eyes. How could people allow others to live like this? Deep down Loren knew that it was time for YWAM to rise up and say, "Enough!"

"How soon do you think we could get a team in here?" Loren turned to ask Gary.

"The sooner the better," Gary replied. "Can you imagine the diseases that sewage is carrying? And did you see the hopeless look in people's eyes? I think we should start with getting a team in to clean up the mess and then see if they will let us hold classes or a medical clinic or something."

"I'll be right behind you," Loren said.

A week later the same group entered a refugee camp in Thailand where many people who had fled Cambodia were housed. On his second day there, Loren walked among the sea of refugees that stretched as far as he could see. A middle-aged Cambodian man saw him coming and beckoned to him. "I am Nghor. Come," he said in heavily accented English. "Come to my house."

Loren followed Nghor as he led him to his "house," which like most of the other places in the camp was merely a square of woven matting on the ground. "My son Sanbaht," he said, pointing to a boy whom Loren guessed was about ten years old.

"Hello," Loren replied. He felt sad for this little man trying to make a dignified life for himself and his son amidst so much chaos. Loren wanted to say something to bring him hope. "Let me tell you about Jesus. He is the Son of God who came down to earth to help us find peace and love."

"I know!" Nghor beamed. "I know Jesus! You know Jesus, too?"

"Yes, I do," Loren exclaimed. "Tell me, how do you know Jesus?"

"An American man told me about him when I lived in Phnom Phen, and I got Him in my heart." Then, unexpectedly, Nghor put his head in his hands and began to weep. "Sanbaht is all I have left. The Khmer Rouge killed my wife and daughters and drove us from our village."

Loren's heart was weighed down, but he knew that the same Christian principles applied all over the world. "You know," he said, "it's very important that we forgive others."

"Yes, I know," Nghor replied. "Jesus forgive me, and I forgive others." Then his face brightened. "You know, twelve hundred Khmer Rouge came into the camp last night! They are over there, in their own section," he said, pointing to the right.

Loren nodded. The refugee camp administrators had told him that when the Khmer Rouge soldiers were being chased, they often stashed their weapons and sought refuge in the safe haven the refugee camps provided. The camps were a safe zone, but they had to keep the Khmer Rouge in a separate, secure area because they were so hated by the other Cambodians.

Nghor continued. "We should go tell them the gospel."

"Yes, we should," Loren agreed as Nghor jumped up and headed toward the barbed-wire compound.

"You say it in English and I will translate for you."

Loren followed, marveling at the man's courage. Nghor actually wanted to preach to the people who had killed his wife and daughters!

Because Loren was a Westerner, the two men were allowed to enter the cordoned-off area where hundreds of Khmer Rouge soldiers sat. The soldiers were all dressed in black, and some of them were very young—just boys.

Loren started preaching, and Nghor stood boldly beside him, translating in a loud voice. After a few minutes, it was obvious who the officers in the group were. They started to get agitated, asserting their authority over the other men, and Loren realized it was time to wrap things up.

"Anyone who wants to know Jesus can follow us to the well," he announced, sensing that things were about to get out of hand.

"Yes, yes, we better go now," Nghor said in an urgent voice. Loren had no idea what would happen next. The tension in the air was electric. Loren half expected someone to take a shot at him as he turned and walked deliberately toward the well.

Once at the well, Loren was excited to find that about fifteen Khmer Rouge men had followed him, right in front of their fellow soldiers! Loren asked Nghor to lead them in a prayer to accept Jesus Christ. At the end of the prayer, Loren looked up to see shining faces. It was an image he knew would not fade from his memory for a long time to come.

By the time Loren got back to Kona, he was convinced that Youth With A Mission was entering a new phase. Not only was the organization to preach the gospel, but also it was to put words into action through mercy.

Gary Stephens gathered a team of thirty enthusiastic young people and headed to Hong Kong, where they started shoveling sewage at the Jubilee refugee camp. Meanwhile Joe Portale led a team to work in the refugee camps in Thailand. This was the two-handed approach at work—offering practical help with one hand and the gospel with the other. Loren had first dreamed of using this approach after witnessing the destruction following Hurricane Cleo in the Bahamas over twenty years before.

The announcement of the official beginning of YWAM Mercy Ministries led to an explosion in volunteers who wanted to train and serve with the organization. All over the world unique new ministries opened up. Two thousand short-term volunteers went and shared their faith behind the Iron Curtain under the able leadership of Al Akimoff. Floyd McClung, who had been with the mission since the first outreach in 1964, moved his family right into the toughest part of Amsterdam. Still others paddled up the Amazon River to share the gospel message with unreached tribes.

In no time at all, eighteen hundred full-time workers were serving around the world with Youth With A Mission. As Loren read their prayer letters and reports, he thought to himself, *This is great, but it is only the beginning. There is so much more to do!*

Chapter 16

New Frontiers

Saturday, December 17, 1983, was an exciting day as Loren and Darlene Cunningham stood with their parents and children waiting for the *Anastasis* to steam into view on the Kona coast of Hawaii.

Twelve-year-old David tugged at Loren's shirtsleeve. "Dad, look, I think that's her."

Shielding his eyes from the sun, Loren peered at the horizon. A puff of smoke hovered over the water and then, almost magically, a huge white ship appeared over the horizon. On cue, outrigger canoes filled with Hawaiian Christians paddled toward the *Anastasis*. People onshore began shouting praises to God, and someone started singing a Hawaiian hymn.

As Loren joined in the chorus, tears sprang to his eyes. He thought back to the all-night prayer meeting in Kaneohe after they had lost the *Maori*. At that meeting they had been convinced that God wanted them to open a different kind of school in Hawaii, that it involved a farm, and that God was going to replace the *Maori* with another, larger, white ship. And now, in the space of ten years it had all come true.

While it was amazing that Youth With A Mission now had its own ship, what was more amazing was that the ship was only one of hundreds of exciting things happening in the mission. Twenty-two years ago there had been Dallas and Larry, and now there were thirty-eight hundred full-time YWAM staff working out of 113 bases in forty nations around the globe. And nearly one thousand of the staff members were from non-Western countries. The *Anastasis* would help many of them bring emergency and medical supplies to the poorest people of the world, along with evangelistic teams to spread the gospel all around the area where the ship docked.

Loren slipped his arm around Darlene's waist, and the two of them watched the ship with the huge YWAM logo emblazoned on its funnel make its way into Kona Bay. It was a storybook scene, one that was, in fact, later captured in a book. The *Anastasis* steaming into Kona became the perfect ending to a book that Loren, with the help of his sister Janice, was writing about the beginning and growth of Youth With A Mission and the spiritual principles he had learned along the way.

The following year, 1984, the book *Is That Really You, God?* was published. It became an instant bestseller, and before long, young and not so young people from all over the world were pouring into YWAM Discipleship Training Schools to take up the challenge of world missions.

The year 1984 also saw the purchase of another ship, the *Good Samaritan*, or the Good Sam, as it was soon affectionately called, and YWAM's Mercy Ships ministry was really on its way.

Toward the end of 1984, Loren was visiting the YWAM base in Salem, Oregon, from which the organization's Slavic Ministries operated. Al Akimoff, who was born in western China while his family was escaping from the Soviet Union, headed up the ministry. Much of the work that Slavic Ministries was involved in was secret because of the severe opposition to Christianity in the Soviet-bloc countries. Bibles and Christian teachings were being smuggled into the Soviet Union at great risk, and Loren was soon to discover that there was something else just as important that Soviet Christians were missing out on. It all started when Al made a comment about the book *Is That Really You, God?*

"You know, Loren," Al said, "you are probably the most famous Christian leader in all of Estonia."

Loren frowned. "How can that be?" he asked. "I have never been to that part of the Soviet Union."

"You haven't, but your book has," Al said with his characteristic smile. "One copy made it across the border a year ago, and a Christian man secretly translated it into Estonian and typed it up with seven pieces of carbon paper under it. That's as many as you can do and still be able to read the copies. Those copies were stapled together and given to Christians to read and hand on. I'm telling you, I think every Christian in Estonia has read your book. And they are all waiting to meet you!"

"Let me pray about it and see what the Lord says," Loren replied.

Six months later, in the early morning calm, Loren Cunningham was sitting in a Russian Lada motorcar being driven through a forest on the edge of Tallinn, Estonia's capital. The driver pulled off into a secluded driveway, at the end of which stood a two-story house. There were no other cars, so the driver parked outside the front door and motioned for Loren to get out and follow him inside.

Loren was surprised to think that he was the first to arrive. He had understood that a group of Christian leaders from all over the Soviet Union were meeting at the house for a week of prayer and encouragement.

The driver, who was an engineer and church leader, seemed to know his way around the house. Loren followed him up a broad flight of stairs and then up a much narrower flight to the attic. A single light bulb burned in the attic, but it was enough to illuminate the faces of thirty or so men who all seemed to be eagerly waiting for Loren to appear.

"It's you! It's really you!" people said as they reached out to kiss Loren on the cheeks and hug him. It took several minutes for the room to settle down, and then Loren was shown to a chair at the front.

Loren looked from one face to the next as the men introduced themselves and, with the help of an interpreter, explained what their ministries were and how God was blessing them under such difficult conditions. When they had finished introducing themselves, one of the men turned to Loren and said, "Tell us what's happening in the world."

"Yes, we have been waiting to hear," another man said.

Loren told them how there were thousands of house churches scattered throughout China and how he had had the opportunity to visit some of the pastors there, just as he was now visiting them. As he spoke, one of the pastors wept, and an old man with a bald head held up his hands to stop Loren for a moment.

"I knew it! I knew it!" the old man said through tears. "I knew God was working in China. The newspapers and the government told us that there were no Christians in China, that everyone there is an atheist. But God's Spirit kept telling me, 'No. They are wrong. I have a people there.'"

Next Loren told them about some of the things he had recently experienced in Africa and Central America. The night went by quickly, and about ten o'clock Loren's escort told him they had to leave.

As the Lada bumped along away from the house, the driver talked to Loren. "I hope you realize what happened in there," he said. "We were living behind a wall of isolation, but today the wall fell, and we can see the world. You *must* continue to do this."

Loren sat in silence for a moment, and then it hit him. *People are living behind walls of isolation all over the world, unaware of what God is doing in other places and among other people. God has given me a unique opportunity to be the eyes and ears in one place and the mouthpiece in another.* From now on, he vowed, everywhere he went he would remember to tell stories about other cultures and lands.

With this goal in mind, in 1985 Loren decided to step down as International Director of Youth With A Mission to devote himself even more to traveling and telling Christians around the world the wonderful things God was doing. Floyd McClung, one of the original YWAMers who had been on the first outreach to the Bahamas, took Loren's place as International Director. Loren retained oversight of training and education, which he believed were two keys to getting the gospel into every place on earth.

Later in 1985 Loren was made aware of a group called the Traveler's Century Club, which was made up of men and women who had been to over 100 of the 315 countries, territories, and nations of the world. As Loren retraced his own steps, he was amazed to discover that he qualified for the club, having visited 180 countries. Now he wanted to go to the rest of the countries he had not yet been to so that he could encourage the Christians he found there and open doors for the work of Youth With

A Mission to take root. As Loren realized that this, too, was what the Lord had said for him to do when he was only thirteen—"Go ye into all the world and preach the gospel"—another piece of his calling fell into place.

All of this kept both Loren and Darlene very busy, and so in early 1986, when they began to notice strange whispered conversations going on around them, they hardly had time to wonder what might be up.

Loren and Darlene did not have to wait long to find out. On a warm Saturday night in November, they were invited to a special evening at the King Kamehameha Hotel in Kona. A stunned Loren stood at the doorway of the banquet room. Inside were about six hundred people, and he knew every one of them! Then he spotted a banner hanging over the stage that read, "Operation Honor."

"That's just what we are here to do." Loren turned to see Floyd McClung smiling at him. "This is our way of saying thank you for all you have done for us in the first twenty-five years of Youth With A Mission."

Loren and Darlene were escorted to the front of the room, and a wonderful evening of stories, songs, and laughter followed. Things could not have been any better when Loren's cousin, Leland Paris, who was now the director of YWAM's work in the Americas, announced, "And now we have a special surprise. Loren and Darlene, would you please step up here."

The couple obediently stepped onto the stage, where Leland presented them with a roll of paper. Loren gingerly unrolled the paper. On it he discovered the blue lines of an architectural plan. Loren looked closer; it was a house plan.

"It's not just any house plan," Al Akimoff announced. "It's *your* house plan!"

Loren stood speechless as Al explained that YWAMers around the world had collected enough money to buy Loren and Darlene a lot about ten blocks above the base in Kona and make a down payment on the house to be built, the one whose plans Loren was holding.

"And that's not all," Al added, pointing at the double doors to their left.

With dramatic flare the doors were swung open to reveal a new bronze-colored Nissan sedan.

"It's for you!" Al announced. "Here are the keys."

Loren's mouth dropped open. Darlene let out a whoop of joy, and they hugged each other.

Loren's mind flashed back to the last car he had owned. It was a 1963 Volkswagen Beetle, which he had sold to go to Switzerland the first time. *How strange it will be to own another car,* he thought.

David then poked his father in the ribs, and Loren knew just what his son was thinking. At fifteen years of age, David had been asking to get his driver's license, and now they had a car for him to drive!

As the night ended, Loren and Darlene were grateful for the wonderful gifts from their friends.

But they were even more grateful for the friends who had come from all over the world to spend the evening with them.

Loren kept busy traveling and speaking as the university at Kona continued to grow and minicampuses were established in various parts of the world. The school changed its name to University of the Nations to reflect the network of courses that were now being taught in many nations and on every continent except Antarctica.

One of these new minicampuses was to be built in the tiny kingdom of Tonga in the South Pacific. The prime minister of Tonga and his wife had donated fifty acres of land for the new campus, and things were going well with the project. A businessman had promised half a million dollars to construct cabins and lecture rooms on the site, and David Triplett, a very qualified developer, was drawing up the plans.

Then in the last week of June 1993, when Loren was preparing to swing through Tonga on his way to Australia, the unexpected happened. Loren received word from the businessman saying that because of difficult circumstances, he no longer had the half million dollars to give to the project. This created quite a problem, as a Leadership Training School had been scheduled to begin at the new campus in September and many of the students attending had already bought their plane tickets to Tonga. Loren decided to go to Tonga anyway, and on June 30 he stood on the site that was to have been the university campus. It was his fifty-eighth birthday, and the YWAM staff in Tonga had made him a cake, which they all ate standing under the lone tree on the otherwise featureless landscape. As Loren looked out over the site, he wondered what would happen next. Where would half a million dollars come from to build the campus?

After spending several days in Tonga, where he had the opportunity to meet with the king, Loren continued on to Australia, where he met up with his parents, who were on a preaching and teaching tour of the country. Now in their eighties, they were as spry as ever.

In Melbourne, Loren watched the Island Breeze team perform. They were a group of Pacific island YWAMers who had formed a cultural dance team and presented a program that showed the progress and blessing of the gospel coming to the islands of the Pacific. When the performance was over, the group crowded around Loren, eager to hear news from Tonga. When they heard that the money for the project had been withdrawn, the members of Island Breeze became quiet.

The next morning Ierusalema, the leader of the group, came to Loren. He held out a check for eighteen thousand Australian dollars.

"Here," he said, "this is the money we had set aside to buy our own place, but it is more important that the islanders have good teaching. You are going to build a campus in Tonga, and we Pacific islanders want to be the first to donate toward it."

Loren gratefully accepted the money. It was not much compared to what was needed, but it was a significant beginning, and he knew it represented a real sacrifice on the part of Ierusalema and his team.

Soon afterward Loren met an old man who announced that he was the great-nephew of Florence Young. Florence was a famous Australian missionary from the 1800s who had worked among the Pacific islanders who were forced to labor in the sugarcane fields around Brisbane, in Queensland. The man was eager to do what he could to help bring Christian education and opportunities to the Pacific islands, and he wrote a check for fifty thousand dollars to go toward the project.

Next two young Australian women, Helen and Penny, who served on the YWAM base in Melbourne, approached Loren with a plan. "You give us all the money you have collected for the Tonga campus and a list of the materials you need, and we'll see what we can get for you. We know a lot of people in town."

Over the next few days, Helen and Penny's progress reports mesmerized the staff at the YWAM base. The two young women went straight to the heads of corporations and explained what Loren needed. Donations and heavily discounted supplies—everything from pots and pans to mattresses, PVC piping, shovels, and faucets—began to pile up at the base. Within a week everything on the list was there—half a million dollars worth of supplies, and all purchased within the budget of sixty-eight thousand dollars! Loren arranged for the supplies to be shipped to Tonga and headed there himself to tell David Triplett the great news.

Since they were now running behind schedule, Loren and the leader of Youth With A Mission in Tonga arranged to rent twenty-one homes in the village of Mu'a. The inhabitants of the homes moved in with relatives so that the YWAMers would all have a place to live. Loren and Darlene and all 250 staff and students slept on the floors of the twenty-one homes. A banana-packing shed was cleaned out for the single men to live in, and the local church served as the lecture room. Mu'a had one drawback, however: no telephone service. Not one of the homes had a working phone, which meant that when people wanted to make or receive a phone call, they had to go into the capital city of Nuku'alofa to the main cable and wireless office. Still, it was a small price to pay for having a place to house the students when they arrived for the Leadership Training School.

As the advance team who had arrived to set up the school prayed, Loren felt strongly that the campus would be ready to move into on October 16, midway through the Leadership Training School. In fact, as he prayed, he saw a picture in his mind of twenty-eight finished cabins, or *fales*, as the Tongans called them, and a twenty-ninth *fale* with three walls completed and a tarp for a roof.

The Leadership Training School began, and midway through September, a month before the deadline that Loren felt he had received in prayer, he asked David Triplett how many *fales* would be ready by October 16.

David shook his head. "We have been having great weather, and as long as it holds, we can have fourteen finished, or possibly fifteen."

Loren smiled. "Well, the Lord told me we are going to have twenty-eight finished, and the twenty-ninth one, which is for Darlene and me, will still be under construction, but livable."

"If that's true, we are going to see a miracle," David said, "because I am telling you that without one, there will be only fifteen *fales* finished at most."

The Leadership Training School continued on, and during work-duty time in the afternoon, the staff and students labored on the buildings. They divided into crews to make more efficient use of their time, with Loren heading up the painting crew.

One day, after finishing painting, Loren returned to the house in Mu'a he was sharing with ten others. As he entered the house, the telephone in the kitchen rang. Loren stared at it for a moment. It was not supposed to be connected! When he picked up the phone, Loren heard the familiar voice of his sister Phyllis. The line was as clear as if she were calling from next door.

"Hi, Loren. I'm glad I got you. I have some bad news. Mom had a stroke this morning. She's resting in the hospital now, but it looks like it was quite a major stroke."

The two of them talked for a few more minutes, and when the call was over, Loren stood and stared at the telephone. How was it that he had received a phone call on a telephone that had no dial tone and had never before rung? He did not even know the phone number! He could not explain it, nor could the owners of the house. But as he prayed that night, Loren said, "God, You are amazing. I am never too far away for You to reach me."

Loren was scheduled to fly back to the United States for a speaking engagement in a few days, and as he prayed, he felt a peace that his mother would still be alive when he got there. Indeed she was, and as Loren returned to Tonga, he was thankful that he had been able to visit her.

Finally October 16 arrived, and sure enough, twenty-eight of the *fales* were finished, and the twenty-ninth had one wall missing and no roof. Someone suggested they throw a tarp over the structure for a roof, and one was found for that purpose.

David Triplett smiled broadly at Loren. "Well, I guess we had our miracle," he said.

Loren nodded.

That day the strangest parade Mu'a had ever witnessed marched from the houses where the students and staff had been staying out to the new University of the Nations campus. Flags and banners waved, and the students sang choruses. And as they marched, Loren's son David filmed the whole event with his movie camera.

Loren and Darlene set up house in the unfinished *fale*, and at two the following morning, rain began to pour down on the tarpaulin. Loren had to run outside and adjust the tarp so that pools of water did not form in the middle of it and cause it to collapse and deluge them. After Loren made the adjustments, the *fale* was fine and did not leak a drop. The Tongan campus was finally up and running!

Chapter 17

Into All the World

Youth With A Mission continued to grow at a fast pace. Loren's book *Is That Really You, God?* had been translated into eighty-two languages, and wherever Loren went, he met Christians who had been challenged to become missionaries after reading it. Loren and Darlene kept busy visiting as many countries as they could, either making way for YWAM to follow or encouraging and helping those who had already set up bases. Sometimes during their travels their lives were in danger, even when on American soil.

On one occasion, Loren was booked on TWA flight 700 from New York's John F. Kennedy Airport to Amsterdam, the Netherlands. As he stepped onto the 747 for the flight, Loren felt God tell him that he was to pray that the plane not take off until something about the flight was revealed. Loren had been on hundreds of flights and had never before received an impression like this one. He obediently stepped into one of the plane's bathrooms and prayed out loud that the plane would go nowhere until whatever it was that needed to be revealed was revealed. After he had prayed, a tired Loren found his assigned seat and stashed his briefcase underneath it. No sooner had he become comfortable in the seat than he fell sleep.

Loren awoke with a start two hours later. He looked out the window of the plane to see that it had not moved an inch. The plane was still at the gate on the ground. At that moment the intercom crackled and the plane's captain began to address the passengers.

"As I have been telling you," the captain began, "this plane has been delayed due to severe storms over Washington, D.C., and Philadelphia. Planes headed there have been diverted to Kennedy Airport, causing the delay. But we have finally been given a slot to take off and hope to be in the air shortly. Again we apologize for the delay. We hope to make up some of the lost time once we are airborne." As he spoke, the plane's engines started.

When the captain had finished speaking, a flight attendant asked the passengers to raise their seats to the upright position and make sure their seatbelts were fastened. Then once more the intercom crackled. It was the captain again. This time his voice sounded urgent.

"Attention all passengers," the captain began. "You are to exit the airplane immediately. Quickly collect your belongings from the overhead lockers and move as fast as you can to the nearest exit. I repeat, exit the plane now. Airline personnel are waiting to escort you to the terminal."

Loren reached under the seat, grabbed his briefcase, and made for the nearest exit, which was behind him. All around, bewildered passengers pushed toward the doors. When they arrived at the terminal, airline agents were posted at the stairs to keep everyone moving. As Loren walked along, the first agent he passed commented, "You sure look relaxed."

Loren replied, "I just woke up from a nap." Then he asked, "Is it a bomb?"

"Yes," the agent replied.

Soon all the passengers were safely inside the terminal, and the captain came to speak to them.

"That was a close call," the captain said, obviously shaken himself. "What happened was that we were delayed on the ground for over two hours, and just as we were about to leave, a call came into the control tower. Assuming the plane had been in the air for two hours, the caller said, 'There's a bomb on Flight TWA 700. The plane is already over the Atlantic, and you can't get it back in time because the bomb is going to explode in thirty minutes.'"

Later, when the captain had finished talking, Loren looked out the terminal window at the special agents swarming over the 747. The agents removed all of the cargo, and soon it was announced that they had found what they were looking for. The airplane would continue on to Amsterdam in three hours.

Some of the passengers were too scared by the whole incident to get back on the airplane, but Loren felt just as calm as he had the first time around. He felt sure that if God could take care of him once, He could do it again.

Loren continued to travel, and by 1999 there were only two countries left that he had not visited—Tristan da Cunha and Libya.

Tristan da Cunha was a tiny island of thirty-seven square miles in the middle of the Atlantic Ocean, at about the same latitude as Buenos Aires, Argentina, and Cape Town, South Africa. It was not easy to get to, but Loren had received an invitation from the Anglican minister to visit and minister on the island. Accompanying him on the trip was Peter Jordan, an ex-Canadian fighter pilot and longtime YWAMer. The two men boarded a 175-foot-long ship in Cape Town. It was the St. Helena mail boat, and once a year it stopped into Tristan da Cunha to deliver mail there as well. Tristan da Cunha was officially the most remote inhabited island on earth, and the captain informed the passengers that if everything went well, they would be there in seven days. About eighty passengers were aboard the ship, among them a doctor who was going to the island to replace the doctor already there.

As the ship bobbed its way across the Atlantic Ocean, Loren learned more about Tristan da Cunha from several of the passengers who had been there before. The island was first inhabited in 1811 and taken over by the British in 1816. The British used it as a naval outpost for a year and then withdrew their men. Several stayed behind, and a few women from St. Helena island to the north married them. Since then an occasional shipwreck survivor or adventure seeker had joined the group, and now seven core families made up the 455 people who lived on the island.

Tristan da Cunha was a volcanic outcrop with steep cliffs and no harbor, a condition that made it impossible to have an airstrip or a commercial wharf. Loren hoped that on this trip the sea would be calm enough for him and Peter to go ashore, especially after a week at sea.

Finally, on a day when the sea was smooth, the craggy outline of Tristan da Cunha came into view. The captain steamed around to the eastern side of the island and dropped anchor. Loren stared at the coastline of the island. He could see a small pier jutting out, flanked by huge, jagged black rocks. Getting a motorboat tied to the pier did not look to him to be an easy task. He would soon find out it was not.

Not everyone onboard the ship was going ashore. Before being allowed to set foot on Tristan da Cunha, a visitor had to have a written invitation to the island. A number of the passengers were waiting to sail on to the next island, Inaccessible Island, to do some bird watching.

A landing boat arrived from the island and was tied to the ship. Loren and Peter climbed down three decks by rope ladder into the boat for the trip to shore. The flat-bottomed boat rocked precariously in the swell as other passengers climbed down the rope ladder into the craft. Once everyone was aboard, the boat was off, cutting a swath through the waves.

To get the boat into the pier required all the skill of the pilot. To get between the rocks that surrounded the pier, the pilot slowed the boat and waited for a large wave. As the wave began to roll in, the pilot hit the throttle, and the boat rode in on the surge of the wave. Once the boat was past the rocks, the pilot quickly maneuvered it behind one of the rocks to avoid being sucked out by the outgoing swell. Loren gazed at huge walruses basking on the rocks around them. When another wave surged in, the pilot hit the throttle once again and guided the boat to the pier, where it was quickly tied up. It was all over in a matter of seconds, but it had been one of the wildest rides of Loren's life.

Once on the island, Loren and Peter enjoyed a wonderful three days staying with the pastor of St. Mary's Church, the only Protestant church on the island. They walked everywhere over the bleak, treeless landscape, visiting people's homes, preaching at the Sunday church service, and teaching Bible studies. When they left Tristan da Cunha, Dr. Truder, who was being replaced, along with his wife and three small sons, left with them.

The doctor was given the cabin next to Loren and Peter, and they all spent a lot of time together on the voyage back to Cape Town. The doctor, who was a vibrant Christian, was not sure what he and his family were going to do next. By the time the ship steamed into the harbor at Cape Town, the Truder family had decided to join Youth With A Mission!

Soon after the trip to Tristan da Cunha, Loren found a way to get into Libya, where he was able to meet with Christian leaders working in the country. Because secret police monitored religious activity, they met secretly. Sharing the gospel with Libyans was illegal, and the last missionary outpost known to the government had been closed in 1960. Loren had now been to every inhabited continent and every country to minister God's love.

By this time the two Cunningham children were grown and had left home. In 1991 Karen graduated from the University of the Nations with a degree in early childhood education. After graduation she moved to Hong Kong, where she worked in a YWAM preschool.

Meanwhile David continued his fascination with the movies. He graduated from the University of the Nations and from the University of Southern California, and then he set about making a career for himself as a film director. In 1995 he married Judy Fitts, a young woman he had met on a YWAM outreach to the Barcelona Olympic Games.

Loren also continued to visit his parents whenever he could. His mother had made a partial recovery from her first stroke, but she had suffered several more. Eventually both Tom and Jewell Cunningham moved to a nursing home in Springdale, Arkansas, near to where Loren's sister Phyllis and her husband, Len, had retired.

By early November 2000, it was obvious to all that Jewell did not have long to live. Loren, along with his father, sisters, and several cousins, rushed to her side. On November 10, they took turns singing and praying as Jewell Cunningham passed away at age ninety-three. As Loren sat looking at his mother's peaceful face, he recalled the many times she had encouraged him to press on in his faith and share the gospel with anyone who would listen. And that is what Loren had tried to do throughout his life.

It was a particularly humid evening in May 2002 as Loren stepped up to a podium to address a group of enthusiastic young Christians, as he had done so many times before, to encourage them as his mother and father had encouraged him. The podium wobbled as Loren placed his notes on it and looked out at the audience. One hundred forty of Youth With A Mission's most promising young leaders sat on folding chairs in the makeshift auditorium. Loren could see glimpses of the night sky through the rusted corrugated iron roof, and white pebbles covered the dirt floor to keep down the dust. Loren was in Barbados, a tiny island in the Caribbean, where Darlene was running a Leadership Training School.

Loren took a breath and began to speak. "I promised that tonight I would answer questions before the lecture. Who has something on his or her mind?"

A hum of voices filled the auditorium as his words were translated into several languages. Then a black man with a thick Caribbean accent stood up. "Loren, could you tell us what excites *you* most about the future of Youth With A Mission?"

A grin spread across Loren's face. Loren loved it when someone asked him about what was on the horizon! He had so much to talk about. He swatted a mosquito away and replied, "That's a great question. Of course, there are many great things going on around the world, and you will all have the opportunity to hear about them while talking to each other at dinner. I see my brother Sargi Abraham from India, who is working with AIDS patients in Georgetown, Guyana, and Braulia Ribeiro, who, along with her husband, Renaldo, heads a wonderful ministry to the tribal people of the Amazon basin. And there's Tavalu, my friend from Tonga, who is working with Genesis, a YWAM communication technology, from the campus in Lausanne, Switzerland. I get excited about what each of you is doing!

"But I suppose if I were to single out one project, it would be the 4 K project. David Hamilton and his team of YWAMers have been working on dividing the entire world into four thousand zones. They have used the best statistics available to group not more than three million people with similar ethnic and national backgrounds into a zone. Then we are going to coordinate a thrust to get a Bible into, and have a missionary personally visit, the homes of all the people living in every zone in the world. We are working to coordinate with thousands of churches and Christian organizations to get this done as fast as possible. We call the zones Omega Zones, because Omega is one of the names of Jesus and because it means 'the last' and we must finish the Great Commission together in this generation.

"There'll be an intranet, too, that will show over two hundred different aspects of each of those zones, from the purity of the water to the prevalence of AIDS, the infant mortality rate, and the number of Christian churches and Bibles in the zone. The new website, www.YWAMconnect.com, will be a great help in planning how to reach these people for Christ and meet their immediate needs as well.

"But what I have been talking about are just tools. Breaking the world into four thousand zones is a tool. Our new YWAMconnect website is a tool. The more than eight hundred YWAM courses in sixty some languages are tools. The hundreds of outreaches and mercy ministries going on around the world right now are tools. They're tools for getting the gospel to everyone on earth. When I was thirteen years old, the Lord came to me and said, "Go into all the world and preach the gospel." Several years later, in Nassau, which is only a few hundred miles from where I am standing today, I saw a vision of waves of young people going out into every continent, every nation, every people group, and to every person to tell them about Jesus Christ. We are called to finish the Great Commission and go into all the world. Together we can do it!"

Bibliography

Cunningham, Jewell Nicholson. *Covered Wagon Days of Evangelism.* Self-published, 1984.

Cunningham, Jewell Nicholson. *Fifty Years of Conflict and Triumph in the Ministry.* Self-published, 1988.

Cunningham, Loren, with Janice Rogers. *Daring to Live on the Edge.* YWAM Publishing, 1991.

Cunningham, Loren, with Janice Rogers. *Is That Really You, God?* YWAM Publishing, 1984, 2001.

Cunningham, Loren, with Janice Rogers. *Making Jesus Lord.* YWAM Publishing, 1988.

Additional material drawn from personal interviews with Loren Cunningham.

About the Authors

Janet and Geoff Benge are a husband and wife writing team with more than thirty years of writing experience. Janet is a former elementary school teacher. Geoff holds a degree in history. Originally from New Zealand, the Benges spent ten years serving with Youth With A Mission. They have two daughters, Laura and Shannon, and an adopted son, Lito. They make their home in the Orlando, Florida, area.

CHRISTIAN HEROES: THEN & NOW are available in paperback, e-book, and audiobook formats, with more coming soon!

www.HeroesThenAndNow.com

Also from Janet and Geoff Benge...

More adventure-filled biographies for ages 10 to 100!

Christian Heroes: Then and Now

Gladys Aylward: The Adventure of a Lifetime • 978-1-57658-019-6
Nate Saint: On a Wing and a Prayer • 978-1-57658-017-2
Hudson Taylor: Deep in the Heart of China • 978-1-57658-016-5
Amy Carmichael: Rescuer of Precious Gems • 978-1-57658-018-9
Eric Liddell: Something Greater Than Gold • 978-1-57658-137-7
Corrie ten Boom: Keeper of the Angels' Den • 978-1-57658-136-0
William Carey: Obliged to Go • 978-1-57658-147-6
George Müller: Guardian of Bristol's Orphans • 978-1-57658-145-2
Jim Elliot: One Great Purpose • 978-1-57658-146-9
Mary Slessor: Forward into Calabar • 978-1-57658-148-3
David Livingstone: Africa's Trailblazer • 978-1-57658-153-7
Betty Greene: Wings to Serve • 978-1-57658-152-0
Adoniram Judson: Bound for Burma • 978-1-57658-161-2
Cameron Townsend: Good News in Every Language • 978-1-57658-164-3
Jonathan Goforth: An Open Door in China • 978-1-57658-174-2
Lottie Moon: Giving Her All for China • 978-1-57658-188-9
John Williams: Messenger of Peace • 978-1-57658-256-5
William Booth: Soup, Soap, and Salvation • 978-1-57658-258-9
Rowland Bingham: Into Africa's Interior • 978-1-57658-282-4
Ida Scudder: Healing Bodies, Touching Hearts • 978-1-57658-285-5
Wilfred Grenfell: Fisher of Men • 978-1-57658-292-3
Lillian Trasher: The Greatest Wonder in Egypt • 978-1-57658-305-0
Loren Cunningham: Into All the World • 978-1-57658-199-5
Florence Young: Mission Accomplished • 978-1-57658-313-5
Sundar Singh: Footprints Over the Mountains • 978-1-57658-318-0
C.T. Studd: No Retreat • 978-1-57658-288-6
Rachel Saint: A Star in the Jungle • 978-1-57658-337-1
Brother Andrew: God's Secret Agent • 978-1-57658-355-5
Clarence Jones: Mr. Radio • 978-1-57658-343-2
Count Zinzendorf: Firstfruit • 978-1-57658-262-6
John Wesley: The World His Parish • 978-1-57658-382-1
C. S. Lewis: Master Storyteller • 978-1-57658-385-2
David Bussau: Facing the World Head-on • 978-1-57658-415-6
Jacob DeShazer: Forgive Your Enemies • 978-1-57658-475-0
Isobel Kuhn: On the Roof of the World • 978-1-57658-497-2
Elisabeth Elliot: Joyful Surrender • 978-1-57658-513-9
D. L. Moody: Bringing Souls to Christ • 978-1-57658-552-8
Paul Brand: Helping Hands • 978-1-57658-536-8
Dietrich Bonhoeffer: In the Midst of Wickedness • 978-1-57658-713-3
Francis Asbury: Circuit Rider • 978-1-57658-737-9

Samuel Zwemer: The Burden of Arabia • 978-1-57658-738-6
Klaus-Dieter John: Hope in the Land of the Incas • 978-1-57658-826-2
Mildred Cable: Through the Jade Gate • 978-1-57658-886-4
John Flynn: Into the Never Never • 978-1-57658-898-7
Richard Wurmbrand: Love Your Enemies • 978-1-57658-987-8
Charles Mulli: We Are Family • 978-1-57658-894-9
John Newton: Change of Heart • 978-1-57658-909-0
Helen Roseveare: Mama Luka • 978-1-57658-910-6
Norman Grubb: Mission Builder • 978-1-57658-915-1
Albert Schweitzer • 978-1-57658-961-8

Heroes of History

George Washington Carver: From Slave to Scientist • 978-1-883002-78-7
Abraham Lincoln: A New Birth of Freedom • 978-1-883002-79-4
Meriwether Lewis: Off the Edge of the Map • 978-1-883002-80-0
George Washington: True Patriot • 978-1-883002-81-7
William Penn: Liberty and Justice for All • 978-1-883002-82-4
Harriet Tubman: Freedombound • 978-1-883002-90-9
John Adams: Independence Forever • 978-1-883002-50-3
Clara Barton: Courage under Fire • 978-1-883002-51-0
Daniel Boone: Frontiersman • 978-1-932096-09-5
Theodore Roosevelt: An American Original • 978-1-932096-10-1
Douglas MacArthur: What Greater Honor • 978-1-932096-15-6
Benjamin Franklin: Live Wire • 978-1-932096-14-9
Christopher Columbus: Across the Ocean Sea • 978-1-932096-23-1
Laura Ingalls Wilder: A Storybook Life • 978-1-932096-32-3
Orville Wright: The Flyer • 978-1-932096-34-7
Captain John Smith: A Foothold in the New World • 978-1-932096-36-1
Thomas Edison: Inspiration and Hard Work • 978-1-932096-37-8
Alan Shepard: Higher and Faster • 978-1-932096-41-5
Ronald Reagan: Destiny at His Side • 978-1-932096-65-1
Davy Crockett: Ever Westward • 978-1-932096-67-5
Milton Hershey: More Than Chocolate • 978-1-932096-82-8
Billy Graham: America's Pastor • 978-1-62486-024-9
Ben Carson: A Chance at Life • 978-1-62486-034-8
Louis Zamperini: Redemption • 978-1-62486-049-2
Elizabeth Fry: Angel of Newgate • 978-1-62486-064-5
William Wilberforce: Take Up the Fight • 978-1-62486-057-7
William Bradford: Plymouth's Rock • 978-1-62486-092-8
Ernest Shackleton: Going South • 978-1-62486-093-5
Benjamin Rush: The Common Good • 978-1-62486-123-9
Dwight Eisenhower: Supreme Commander • 978-1-62486-142-0

Available in paperback, e-book, and audiobook formats.
Unit Study Curriculum Guides are available for many biographies.
www.YWAMpublishing.com